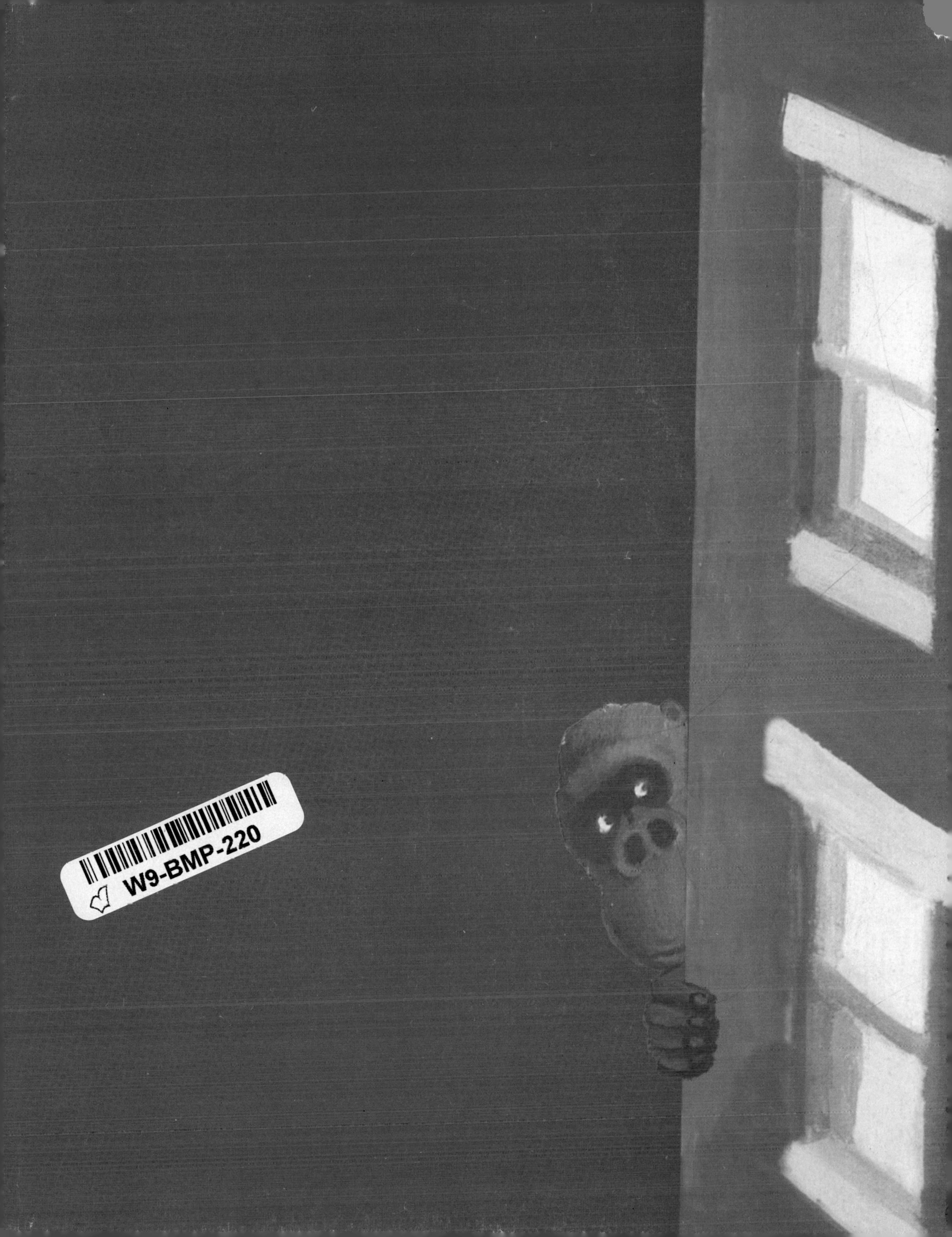

PICTURE IT!

A Comprehension Handbook

Author's Purpose

To Persuade

To Inform

To Entertain

To Express Emotion

An author's purpose is the reason an author has for writing.

Cause and Effect

classify and categorize

Classifying or categorizing means putting things that are related into groups.

Forest Life

Desert Life

Compare and Contrast

As you read, think about what is alike and what is different.

Alike

Different

Draw Conclusions

Combine what you already know with new information to draw conclusions.

What I know:

Riding uphill can make you tired.
Sometimes your face scrunches up when you work hard.
Exercise can make you feel warm.

Conclusion:

The girl is becoming hot and tired.

Fact and Opinion

A statement of fact can be proven true or false.
A statement of opinion tells someone's ideas or feelings.

Generalize

Main Idea and Details

What is the selection all about? What details support the main idea?

Graphic Sources

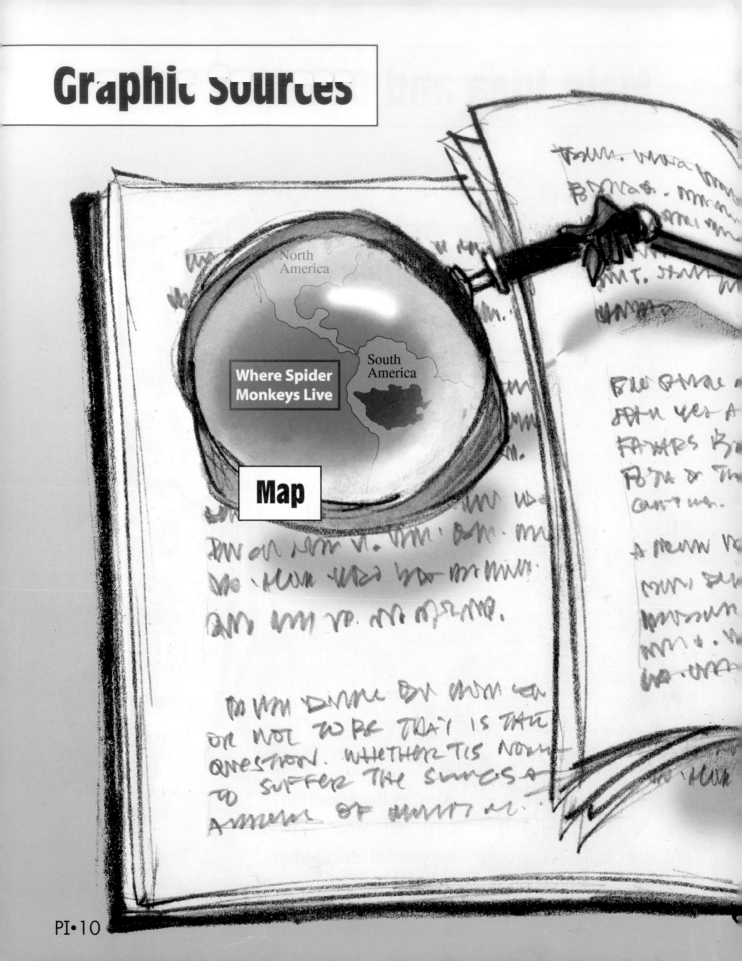

North America

South America

Where Spider Monkeys Live

Map

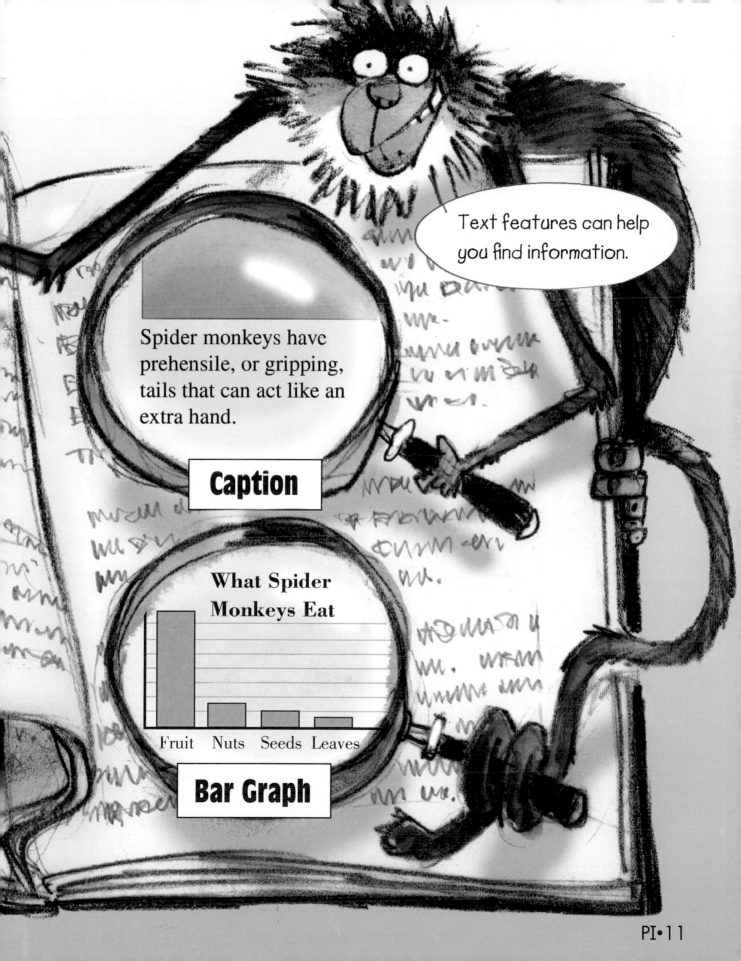

Literary Elements

Characters

A character is a person or animal in a story.

Setting

The setting is the time and place in which a story happens.

Plot

A story's plot is the important events that happen.
The plot starts with a problem and ends with a solution.

Theme

The theme is the big idea of a story.

Sequence

The sequence of a selection is the order of events.

First

Next

Last

Steps in a Process

Reading STREET

Program Authors

Peter Afflerbach

Camille Blachowicz

Candy Dawson Boyd

Connie Juel

Edward Kame'enui

Donald Leu

Jeanne Paratore

Sam Sebesta

Deborah Simmons

Alfred Tatum

Sharon Vaughn

Susan Watts Taffe

Karen Kring Wixson

PEARSON

Glenview, Illinois • Boston, Massachusetts • Chandler, Arizona
Shoreview, Minnesota • Upper Saddle River, New Jersey

Living and Learning

Which skills help us make our way in the world?

18

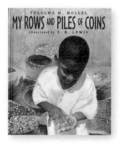

Contents

Get Online!
PearsonSuccessNet.com

Smart Solutions

THE BIG **?** What are smart ways that problems are solved?

New Literacies ▶ e-mail/social studies

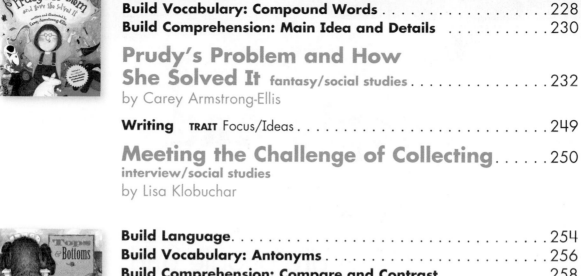

Picture It! A Comprehension Handbook **PI•1–PI•15**
Words! A Vocabulary Handbook **W•1–W•15**

UNIT 3 Contents

People and Nature

 How are people and nature connected?

22

Picture It! A Comprehension Handbook PI•1–PI•15
Words! A Vocabulary Handbook W•1–W•15

Get Online!

PearsonSuccessNet.com

See It!
- Concept Talk Video
- *Picture It!* Animation
- e-Books

Hear It!
- Selection Snapshot and Response
- Paired Selection e-Text
- Grammar Jammer
- e-Books

Do It!
- Online Journal
- Story Sort
- New Literacies Activity
- Success Tracker

Living and Learning

Which skills help us make our way in the world?

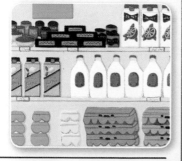

Living and Learning

Let's Talk About
Trying New Things

LS1.7 Use clear and specific vocabulary to communicate ideas and establish the tone.

27

Build Vocabulary

Learn ◉ **Skill Homographs** are words that are spelled the same but have different meanings. Homographs may or may not be pronounced the same. For example, *bat* means "a stick used to hit a ball." *Bat* also means "a flying animal." When you see a word you know but the meaning doesn't make sense, look at the nearby words and sentences. They may help you find the correct meaning of a homograph.

Practice Read "The Inventor" on page 29. As you read, look for words that might be homographs. Look at the nearby words to figure out the meaning that makes sense.

Words to Know	vision	bat	battery
	plug	fuel	term
	blew		

On Your Own Reread "The Inventor." Make a list of the homographs you find. Then write both meanings of each word. Use your glossary or a dictionary if you need help.

R1.4 Use knowledge of antonyms, synonyms, homophones, and homographs to determine the meanings of words. **R1.6** Use sentence and word context to find the meaning of unknown words.

The Inventor

Max liked to invent things. He spent a lot of time working on projects in his lab. His neighbors admired his vision and creativity, but their children thought he was strange. They told each other that he kept a bat as a pet. They stayed out of his yard.

One hot summer day, Max had a terrific idea. He wanted to create something the children would enjoy. It would not need a battery. It would not plug into the wall or use fuel such as gasoline. Max's invention would run on a special kind of power—kid power!

Max wanted to use the invention soon, so he set a short term for the project. He worked day and night to finish. When the amazing "Summer Splasher" was ready, Max set it up in his front yard. Some children stopped to ask Max what it was. He showed them how to jump on the big pedal to pump water through the sprinkler. This also made the fan move. A cool breeze blew across the yard. Soon the children were lining up to try it out.

⏸ Need a Review?
See *Words!*, p. W•10 for more information about homographs.

▶ Ready to Try It?
Read *When Charlie McButton Lost Power*, pp. 32–49.

When Charlie McButton Lost Power

Living and Learning

Build Comprehension

Learn ⊙ **Skill Character and Setting**

- A character is a person or animal in a story.

- Authors usually describe characters, but they do not tell everything. You can learn more about characters from their actions and what they say.

- The setting is when and where a story takes place.

- An author may tell you the setting, or you may figure it out from details in the story.

Practice Read "Flash to Bang" on page 31. Look for details that help you understand the characters and setting.

Story Title	
Characters	Setting

On Your Own **Write to Read** Reread "Flash to Bang." Make a chart like the one above. Write details from the story that tell about the characters and the setting. Then write a paragraph explaining how the setting affects Thomas's actions and behaviors.

 Need a Review?
See *Picture It!*, p. PI·12 for more information about character and setting.

▷ **Ready to Try It?**
As you read *When Charlie McButton Lost Power*, pp. 32–49, watch for details that tell about the characters and setting.

🐻 **R3.3** Determine what characters are like by what they say or do and by how the author or illustrator portrays them.

Flash to Bang

Thomas stood in the yard and looked up at a big dark cloud. He could see lightning in the distance. It would probably rain soon. All week the weather had been sunny and warm. Now it was Saturday—no school, no karate practice, no piano lesson—and he really wanted to spend the day playing outside.

"Why can't I stay outside?" he asked his mom. "I don't mind getting wet."

"It's not the rain I'm worried about," she told him as they went inside. "Lightning is dangerous, and the storm is coming closer."

"How can you tell?" Thomas wanted to know.

"Lightning causes thunder," his mom replied. "But it takes time for the sound of the thunder to reach us." She then explained the Flash-to-Bang method of figuring out how far away the lightning strikes were. "When you see a flash of lightning," she continued, "count the seconds until you hear the thunder. For every five seconds you count, the lightning is about one mile away."

During the storm, they sat together by the window and counted. Being indoors on a weekend wasn't so bad after all. Thomas learned something new and had fun with his mom.

Skill The first paragraph tells the setting, or where Thomas is. It also gives a clue about Thomas's character—he is busy during the week and doesn't have much free time.

Skill Notice how the setting and the characters are connected. Here, when the setting changes, Thomas changes his actions.

When Charlie McButton Lost Power

Author: Suzanne Collins
Illustrator: Mike Lester

**What does Charlie do
when he loses power?**

Charlie McButton had likes and like-nots.
The things that he liked involved handsets and bots,
Computerized games where he battled bad creatures.
The things he liked-not didn't have blow up features.

Then one day a thunderstorm blew into town
And brought his tech empire tumbling down.
A lightning bolt struck an electrical tower,
And Charlie McButton?
     His whole world lost power.

He looked left, he looked right, and his heart
filled with dread.

The TV, the lights and his clock were all dead.

He jumped to his feet, his lungs gasping for air.

The room spun around and he clung to his chair.

He tried to cry "Help!" but
just managed a squeak.

The blackout had blacked
out his power to speak.

Thank goodness his mother
had ears like a bat.

She came to his room and
she gave him a pat.

Help!

"Oh, Charlie," she said, picking up on his fears,
"The lights will come back when the bad weather clears.
You'll have to find something without plugs to play.
Read a book!
Clean your room!
Sing a song!
Model clay!"

Could *anything* be any duller than clay?
Soggy gray clay on a soggy gray day?
He hated the way the clay got under his nails
And how he could only make snowmen and snails.

He dove for a gadget he'd outgrown last spring.
It was handheld, outdated, not much of a thing.
But he clutched the old toy like a lifeline that day.
See, it ran on one battery. The size? Triple-A.

He flicked the On/Off switch to On double quick,
But no happy humming sound followed the click.
He unlatched a hatch and his blood turned to ice.
"The battery is gone from my backup device!"

World records were set in the ten-meter dash
As away down the hallway he flew like a flash,
Seeking one battery, just one triple-A
That would rescue one boy from a gray day of clay.

But just when his search nearly drove him insane,
He ran past the bedroom of Isabel Jane.
His three-year-old sister was happily walking
A doll back and forth, and the doll—it was talking!

Now, dolls didn't talk on their own as a rule.
They needed a power source, some kind of fuel.
In less than a second he'd made his decision.
Call it bad judgment, a real lack of vision.

Somehow his head didn't warn of his folly,
And Charlie McButton…

He pounced on that dolly.
He plucked out his prize through the baby doll's dress,
And Isabel Jane made a sound of distress.

It was just a short walk to the foot of the stair
Where resided the McButton time-out time chair.
To add to the fun of his term in the seat,
Isabel Jane came to play at his feet.

And Isabel Jane, the Battery Queen,
Had more triple-A's than he'd ever seen.
They powered her puppies, they powered her clocks,
They powered her talkative alphabet blocks.

Assaulted by nonstop mechanical chatter,
Charlie McButton got madder and madder.
He snapped at his sis from his time-out time zone,
"How come you can't ever

just

leave

me

alone!"

Her eyes filled with tears and she gave them a rub.
She went to the bathroom and hid in the tub.
Then Charlie McButton felt totally rotten
And couldn't help thinking some things he'd forgotten.

Mainly he thought that, for sisters that toddle,
Isabel Jane was a pretty good model.
She clearly adored him. She didn't have fleas.
At dinner she'd secretly eat up his peas.

And sometimes—although he'd most hotly deny it—
He liked to just sit there beside her in quiet.
Wrapped up in a blanket, watching TV,
Her head on his shoulder, her foot on his knee.

He sat and he thought and he stared at the rain.
When his time-out was done, he found Isabel Jane.
From the edge of the tub she gave him a peek,
So he said, "Hey, are we playing hide-and-go-seck?"

She was happy at once and ran into the hall,
As she loved playing hide-and-go-seek most of all.
They took turns being "It" and counting to ten.
They hid in the plants and the guinea pig pen.

45

And when he found Isabel Jane in her quilt,
They decided a big blanket fort should be built.
Then the gloom made him think
about dragons and spells....
So Charlie became the great wizard McSmells.
And Isabel Jane, who desired a role,
Magically changed to his faithful old troll.

Between tracking down dragons and brewing up lizards
And handling the day-to-day business of wizards,
Like forging his faithful old troll a new sword,
Charlie McButton forgot to be bored.

At supper they ate under real candlelight.
The daytime had melted right into the night.
And after they'd all been asleep for an hour…
The world came alive with a big surge of power.
Oh, it's finally back, Charlie thought with a grin.
Tomorrow I'll wake up and I can plug in!

But another thought hit him he couldn't explain:
I might *also* find dragons with Isabel Jane.

Think, Talk and Write

Talk About It Look back at the pictures in this story. How do they help tell the story? Is there one picture that especially helped you understand how Charlie felt? Tell why.

1. Use the pictures below to retell the story. **Retell**

2. How would you describe Charlie? What details from the story helped you describe him? How would Charlie have acted differently if the power had not gone out? **Character and Setting**

3. Think of someone you know who is like Charlie. In what ways does that person remind you of Charlie? **Prior Knowledge**

4. Some of the Words to Know on p. 28 are homographs and have more than one meaning. Look for other words in *Charlie McButton* that have multiple meanings. **Vocabulary**

TEST PRACTICE

Look Back and Write Look back at the question on page 33. Think about how Charlie acts when the power first goes out and what he does later in the story. Now write a paragraph explaining the changes in Charlie's behavior.

Meet author **Suzanne Collins** on page **448** and illustrator **Mike Lester** on page **449**.

Retell

R3.3 Determine what characters are like by what they say or do and by how the author or illustrator portrays them.

Writing

Prompt *When Charlie McButton Lost Power* is a narrative poem about a boy who tries something new. Think about what it would be like to lose power at home. Now write a narrative poem telling about that time.

Writing Trait

Careful **word choice** makes writing interesting.

Student Model

Blackout

One evening last summer,
The power went out.
My brother and sister were scared.

I got out a flashlight
And turned it on bright.
"Do not be afraid!" I declared.

We made shadow puppets
And stayed up too late.
By morning the lights were repaired.

A sentence begins with a capital letter and has end punctuation.

A poem usually has regular rhyme and rhythm.

The writer chooses rhyming words to give the poem style.

Use the model to help you write your own narrative poem.

R3.5 Recognize the similarities of sounds in words and rhythmic patterns (e.g., alliteration, onomatopoeia) in a selection. **LS1.4** Identify the musical elements of literary language (e.g., rhymes, repeated sounds, instances of onomatopoeia).

Living and Learning

Sequence is a text structure authors use to show the order in which events happen. Recognizing the text structure can help you to remember important points the author makes. Look for clue words that signal sequence, such as *before*, *then*, *at first*, and *soon after*.

 Ready to Try It?
Read *How a Kite Changed the World.* Look for clue words to help you identify the sequential text structure.

Science Link

Ben Franklin is just one of many scientists who have done important research about electricity. Use the library or the Internet to find out more about Thomas Edison, Michael Faraday, or another scientist. If you search the Internet, try using the phrase "electricity time line" as your keyword.

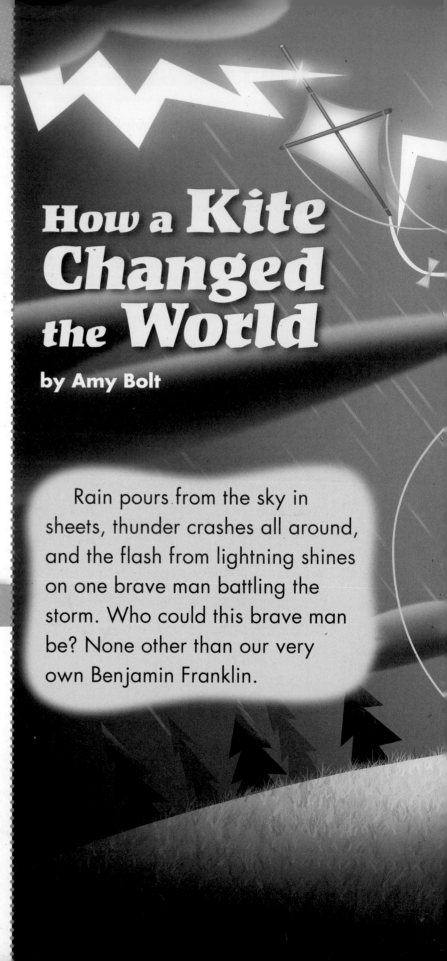

How a Kite Changed the World

by Amy Bolt

Rain pours from the sky in sheets, thunder crashes all around, and the flash from lightning shines on one brave man battling the storm. Who could this brave man be? None other than our very own Benjamin Franklin.

Benjamin Franklin believed that thunderclouds carried electricity and that lightning was a large flash of electricity. He wondered if electricity could be useful and if it could, how? Benjamin Franklin also wanted to find a way to protect houses from getting hit by lightning. That is why one stormy night Benjamin Franklin stood in the middle of a field, holding a kite.

On that famous night, Benjamin Franklin held a kite with a metal rod about a foot long placed on top of it. Benjamin Franklin believed that this rod would catch lightning. He tied to the string of the kite a metal key. If his theory was right, the electricity would travel to the key.

Benjamin Franklin took the kite to an open field. When the wind started to blow, he let the kite fly. He watched the kite and waited. Benjamin Franklin was starting to get tired and he began to think that his plan was not going to work. Then he noticed that some loose bits of kite string were standing very straight. It was working! He touched the key with the back of his hand and felt a shock. Electricity had passed from the cloud to the kite to the key.

This was not the end of Benjamin Franklin's tests of electricity. He turned his house into a laboratory by putting lightning bells in place. The bells rang when lightning was nearby.

Benjamin Franklin fixed a tall metal rod on his roof to attract the lightning. The rod would attract the electric current in the air and travel through a wire in his home. Small bells and brass balls hung from the wire. When clouds passed with electricity in them, the balls would strike the bells, the bells would ring, and a flash of electricity would travel between them.

From his experiments with the lightning bells, Benjamin Franklin hoped to show that placing a lightning rod on the roof of a building might save it from damage. If the lightning rod would attract lightning for Benjamin Franklin's experiments, then the rod could also redirect lightning away from buildings.

At first, many people were interested in Benjamin Franklin's discoveries. But they did not stay interested for a long time. To most people, watching his tests was like watching a show. The sparks, lights, and bells were fun to look at, but people didn't understand why electricity was important. With time, people began to pay more attention to ideas about electricity and how it may benefit their lives.

Before Benjamin Franklin and his kite, people knew very little about lightning and electricity. Benjamin Franklin took something found in nature, electricity, and explored everything about it. Today, every time we turn on a light we know that Benjamin Franklin's ideas about electricity were right.

Reading Across Texts

Over time, Benjamin Franklin's experiments with electricity changed how people lived. If Charlie McButton could talk to Benjamin Franklin about electricity, what do you think Charlie would say?

Writing Across Texts Pretend you are Charlie. Write a letter to Benjamin Franklin telling him what you think of his experiments with electricity.

Let's Talk About
Trading With One Another

LS1.7 Use clear and specific vocabulary to communicate ideas and establish the tone.

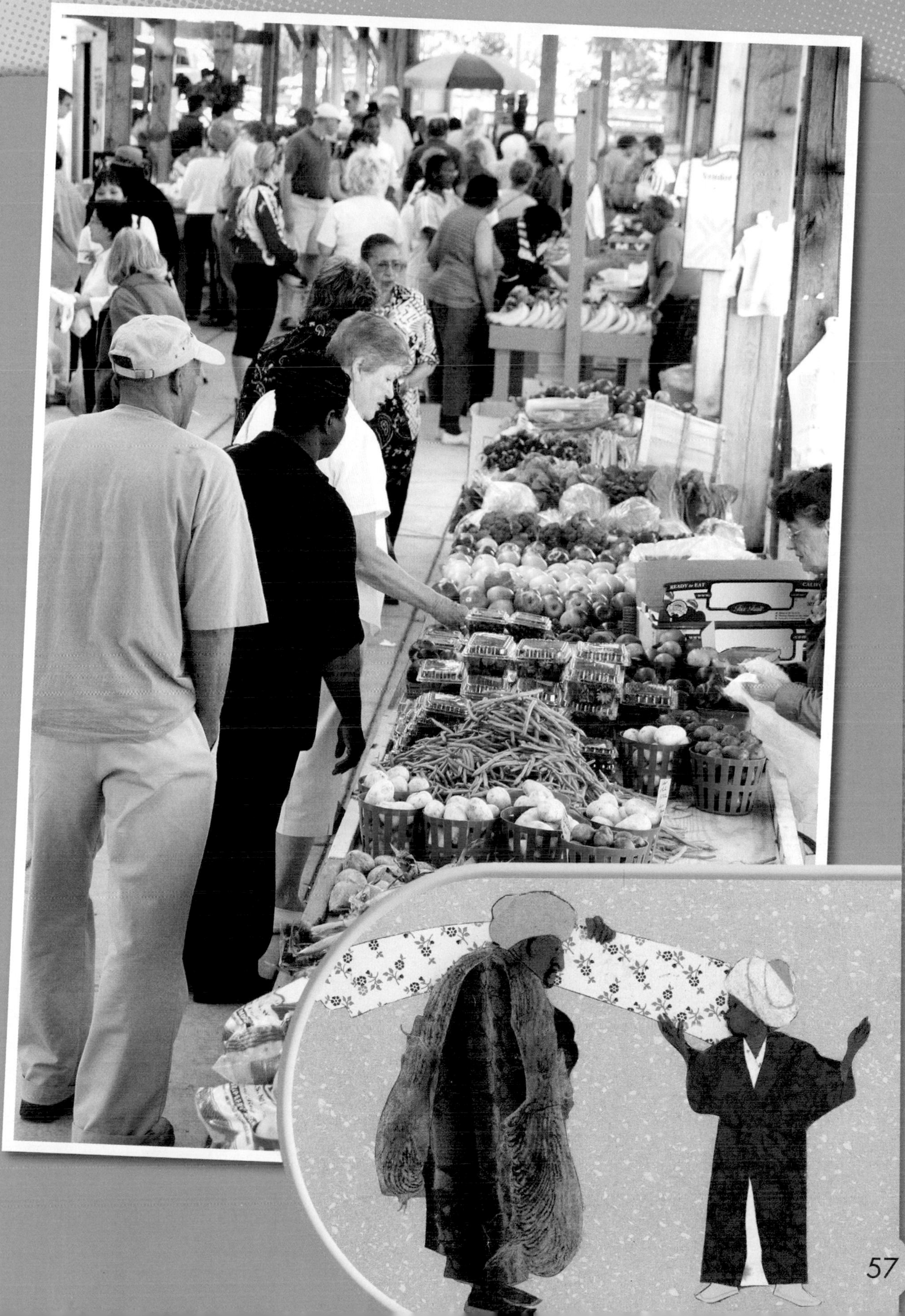

Build Vocabulary

Learn ⊙ **Skill Compound Words** are made up of two smaller words put together. To find the meaning of a compound word, think of the meaning of each smaller word. Then put the two meanings together. For example, a *goatseller* is a person who sells goats.

Practice Read "At the Market" on page 59. As you read, study the highlighted words. Decide which words are compound words. Make a list of the compound words you find.

Words to Know	marketplace	straying	carpenter
	plenty	merchant	thread
	carpetmaker	knowledge	

On Your Own Reread "At the Market." Look at your list of compound words. Think about the meanings of the small words in each compound word. Then write the meaning of the compound word.

G2R1.8 Use knowledge of individual words in unknown compound words to predict their meaning.

At the Market

Imagine a small town in Europe three hundred years ago. It is market day. People come from miles around to buy and sell things. They meet in the marketplace in the center of the town. Look, there is a farmer who has come to sell his fruits and vegetables. And here is another farmer who is selling chickens and geese. He has put them in wicker cages to keep them from straying. The carpenter has made chairs and tables for people's homes. The baker has baked plenty of pies, cakes, and breads. This merchant sells things for sewing—cloth, needles, and thread. And over there is a carpetmaker. He has made beautiful carpets.

People walk from stall to stall looking at the items. They know what they are willing to pay, and they use this knowledge to decide what they will buy.

Is it different from today? Not really. Just think about your last trip to a modern marketplace—the shopping mall!

 Need a Review?
See *Words!*, p. W•9 for more information about compound words.

 Ready to Try It?
Read *What About Me?*, pp. 62–75.

Build Comprehension

Learn   ⊙ **Skill Sequence**

- Sequence is the order in which things happen in a story—what happens first, next, and last.

- Sometimes a writer uses clue words like *first, next,* and *in the morning*. These words can help you understand the order of events in the story.

- If there are no clue words, you can try picturing in your mind what is happening.

Practice   Read "Chores" on page 61 to find out what happens first, next, and last.

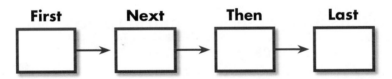

| **First** | **Next** | **Then** | **Last** |

On Your Own   **Write to Read** Reread "Chores." Make a sequence diagram to keep track of the most important events. Use the diagram to help you write a summary of the story.

 Need a Review?
See *Picture It!*, p. PI•14 for more help with sequence.

▷ **Ready to Try It?**
As you read *What About Me?*, pp. 62–75, pay attention to the sequence of events.

 G5R2.2 Analyze text that is organized in sequential or chronological order.

Chores

Louisa looked at the Chores list. It was her turn to fold the laundry. That was the chore she hated most. How could she get out of it?

Louisa saw her brother J. B. in his room. "J. B., would you like to make some money?" Louisa asked.

"What's the catch?" asked J. B.

"I'll pay you 50 cents to fold the …," Louisa stopped. She remembered that she had spent her 50 cents yesterday. "Never mind."

Next Louisa saw her sister Grace pouting in the living room.

"I got the worst chore on the list today," said Grace. "I hate dusting furniture!"

"Dusting furniture isn't bad. I have to fold the laundry! *That's* the worst!" Louisa said.

"I don't mind folding laundry," said Grace. "Anything but dusting!"

The two girls looked at each other. They both smiled. As Grace folded the laundry, Louisa hummed and dusted.

Skill Here Louisa stops talking in the middle of her sentence. That helps tell the order of events. First Louisa remembers she doesn't have money to pay J. B. Then she tells him, "Never mind."

Skill Here's a clue word that helps tell the order of events. What happens after Louisa talks to J. B.?

Genre

A **fable** is a story that teaches a lesson, or moral.
What moral does this story teach?

What About Me?

by Ed Young

Who asks, "What about me?"
and why does he or she ask it?

Once there was a boy who wanted knowledge, but he did not know how to gain it. "I shall see a Grand Master," he said. "He has plenty. Perhaps he will give me some."

When he arrived, he bowed and said, "Grand Master, you are wise. How may I gain a little bit of your knowledge?"

The Grand Master said, "You need to bring me a small carpet for my work." The boy hurried off to find a carpetmaker.

"Carpetmaker," he said, "I need a small carpet to give to the Grand Master for his work."

The carpetmaker barked, "He has needs! What about me? I need thread for weaving my carpets. Bring me some thread, and I will make you a carpet."

So the boy went off to find a spinner woman.
He found her at last. "Spinner Woman," he said, "I need some thread for the carpetmaker, who will make me a carpet to give to the Grand Master for his work."

"You need thread!" she wheezed. "What about me? I need goat hair to make the thread. Get me some and you can have your thread."

So the boy went off looking for someone who kept goats.

When he came to a goatkeeper, the boy told him his needs. "Your needs! The others' needs! What about me? You need goat hair to buy knowledge—I need goats to provide the hair! Get me some goats, and I will help you."

The boy ran off again to find someone
who sold goats. When he found such a man, the boy
told him of his problems, and the goatseller said,
"What do I know about thread or carpets or Grand
Masters? I need a pen to keep my goats in—they are
straying all over the place! Get me a pen, and you can
have a goat or two."

The boy's head buzzed. "Everyone has a need," he mumbled to himself as he hurried off. "And what of my need for knowledge?" But he went to a carpenter who made pens, and he gave the carpenter his long story.

"Say no more," the carpenter said. "Yes, I make pens, but I need a wife, and no one will have me. Find me a wife, and we can talk about your problems."

So the boy went off, going from house to house.

Finally he met a matchmaker. "Yes, I know such a girl—she will make a good wife, but I have a need. All my life, I have wanted. . . . "

"Yes?" said the boy.

"Knowledge," said the matchmaker. "Bring me knowledge, and I will give you the young girl's name to take to the carpenter."

The boy was stunned. "But . . . but we cannot get knowledge without a carpet, no carpet without thread, no thread without hair, no hair without a goat, no goat without a pen, no pen without a wife for the carpenter."

"Stop!" said the matchmaker. "I for one don't want knowledge that bad." And she sent the boy away.

"I need a carpet," the boy chanted. "I need a carpet, I NEED A CARPET!"

And so he began to wander farther and farther from his village.

Until one day he came to a village where he saw a merchant in the marketplace, wringing his hands.

"Merchant," the young man said, "why do you wring your hands?"

The merchant looked at the young man's gentle face. "I have an only and beautiful daughter who I think is mad. I need help, but I don't know where to find it."

"I could not even get a piece of thread when I wanted it," said the young man. "But perhaps I can help."

And so the merchant led him to the girl. When she saw his kind face, she stopped ranting. "Oh, good young man," she said, "I have a need. My father wishes me to marry a merchant like himself, but I love a simple carpenter."

When she described the carpenter, the wanderer suddenly said, "Why, she loves the very carpenter I know!" And so he went to the other village and took the girl and her secret to him.

In thanks, the carpenter immediately gave the young man wood for a pen.

The goatseller placed the goats in the pen and gave him some goats, which he took to the goatkeeper, who gave him some of their hair, which he took to the spinner, who spun him thread.

Then he took the thread to the carpetmaker, who made a small carpet.

This small carpet he carried back to the Grand Master. When he arrived at the house of the wise man, he gave the carpet to him.

"And now, Grand Master, may I have knowledge?"

"But don't you know?" said the Grand Master. "You already have it."

The Grand Master's Morals are Two:

Some of the most precious gifts that we receive are those we receive when we are giving.

and

Often, knowledge comes to us when we least expect it.

Think, Talk and Write

Talk About It The boy in this story tells about finding knowledge. Tell a story of how you found knowledge.

1. Use the pictures below to retell the story. **Retell**

2. What is important about the sequence in which this story takes place? **Sequence**

3. What did you predict would happen when the boy met the matchmaker? Did your prediction change as you read? If so, why? **Predict**

4. Draw a map of the boy's journey. Label each stop with the name of the character he visits. Circle the compound words. Can you think of other compound words that name jobs people have? **Vocabulary**

Look Back and Write Find three places in the story where a character asks, "What about me?" Think about why the characters ask the boy this question. Now write a response to the question on page 63.

Meet author and illustrator Ed Young on page 451.

Retell

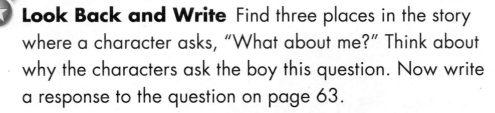

R2.4 Recall major points in the text and make and modify predictions about forthcoming information.

Writing

Prompt *What About Me?* is a fable about a boy who learns a lesson while trading. Think about a lesson you have learned. Now write a fable that teaches that lesson.

Writing Trait

Use proper **spelling** and **punctuation** to make your writing easy to read.

Student Model

An Important Lesson

Cat and Dog are playing together. Dog is eating some cookies, but he does not offer any to Cat. "I'm hungry," Cat says. "Will you please share your snack with me?"

Dog says, "No. I'm too hungry." Cat feels sad.

Later Dog asks Cat to share her toy. What will Cat do? Maybe she will not share her toy, just as Dog didn't share his snack.

Cat says, "Last time we played together, you didn't share your snack. That made me sad, and I don't want you to feel sad now. So I will share my toy with you."

Dog learned an important lesson that day: Treat others the way you want to be treated.

Cat and Dog are the subjects of the sentence.

Correct punctuation clarifies meaning.

The moral, or lesson, is clearly stated at the end of a fable.

Living and Learning

Use the model to help you write your own fable.

G2LC1.5 Use quotation marks correctly. **W2.1b** Write narratives: Include well-chosen details to develop the plot.

Author's Purpose is the author's reason for writing. An author may write to inform or entertain readers. *Carpet-Weaving* is written in two parts. Do you think the author has two different purposes for writing?

Ready to Try It?
As you read *Carpet-Weaving*, think about how the author's purpose seems to change. Why would the author change purposes?

Social Studies Link

Although carpets originated in Eastern cultures, they are now made all over the world. Use the Internet or the library to search for examples of other goods that originated somewhere else and are now widely made. Share your results with your class.

Carpet-Weaving
By Emily Zink Kirchner

Carpet-weaving is an ancient art form that is important in Eastern cultures. Handmade rugs are both useful and beautiful. From Turkey to China these carpets or rugs, have covered walls, floors, and furniture, and have even been used as curtains to divide rooms. They have also been placed under saddles for centuries.

Rugs are usually made out of goat hair, wool, or cotton. Carpetmakers, sit at looms and tie knots by hand around vertical pieces of yarn. Hand-knotted rugs can have 1,000 knots in a square inch (about the size of a stamp). It can take over a year for one person to make a rug!

Carpetmakers use patterns that look like animals and plants. Sometimes the rugs have symbols that represent power, strength, or long life.

Eastern literature is filled with stories about these beautiful rugs. One famous book called *1001 Nights,* or *Arabian Nights,* tells the story of a magic carpet.

Three princes were looking for gifts in a contest to win the hand of the princess they each loved. The first prince traveled to a faraway town and rested in a marketplace. A carpet dealer came by, carrying an average-looking rug.

"40,000 gold pieces for this rug," he called.

The prince was shocked at the price and asked, "Who would buy this rug at such a high price?"

"This is a magic carpet, sir," said the dealer. "Whoever sits on this rug will be immediately taken to the place he wishes to go without delay."

The prince gave the dealer the gold pieces, for surely this flying carpet would win for him the hand of the princess. The second prince found a tube of ivory through which he could see anything his heart desired. And the third Prince found an apple that could heal any sickness just by its smell.

On the way home, the three princes compared their gifts. When the second prince looked into his ivory tube, he saw their beloved princess, sick and dying. So the third prince showed them the apple that healed all diseases. Then the first prince pulled out his flying carpet. The three princes climbed on and magically flew to save their beloved.

None of the princes won the princess's hand because each one's gift was needed to help save her life.

Reading Across Texts

What About Me? and *Carpet-Weaving* teach the importance of cooperation. How do the characters work together? What would happen if the characters choose not to help each other?

Writing Across Texts Rewrite the end of the story as if no one worked together.

Let's Talk About

Achieving Goals

Build Vocabulary

Learn ⦿**Skill Unfamiliar Words** Sometimes when you are reading, you may see a word you do not know. You can use a glossary or a dictionary to find the meaning of that word. A glossary appears at the back of a book. It lists important words from that book and their meanings. A dictionary is a separate book that lists words and their meanings, as well as other information about the words.

Practice Read "First Snow" on page 85. As you read, make a list of the highlighted words. Use the glossary at the back of this book or a dictionary to find the meaning of each word. Write the meaning next to each word on your list.

Words to Know	splendid	gear	willow
	yanked	parka	twitch

On Your Own Reread "First Snow." Look back at your list of vocabulary words and their meanings. Now write a short paragraph using three vocabulary words.

R1.7 Use a dictionary to learn the meaning and other features of unknown words. **R2.1** Use titles, tables of contents, chapter headings, glossaries, and indexes to locate information in text.

First Snow

Jack and Missy had never seen snow. They lived in Florida. The weather there was too warm for snow. Then last winter they visited their cousins in Michigan.

On the second day of their visit, a snowstorm brought seven inches of the splendid white stuff. Hooray! Jack and Missy borrowed their cousins' extra boots and other outdoor gear. Then they all ran outside to play.

In the yard, the willow trees looked like they were made of snow. All the branches were covered in white. Missy went closer for a better look. Just then Jack yanked one of the branches. The snow poured down onto Missy's head. Some fell inside the neck of her parka. Brrr! The cold made her twitch and shiver, but she laughed anyway.

They took turns pulling each other in the sled. They made a snowman. Finally they were too cold and wet to stay outside. They went inside for dry clothes.

Jack and Missy had fun playing in the snow all week. By the end of the visit, though, they were glad to go back to the sunshine of Florida.

 Need a Review?
See *Words!*, p. W·14 for more help on using your dictionary or glossary to find the meanings of unfamiliar words.

 **Ready to Try It?**
Read *Kumak's Fish*, pp. 88–103.

Build Comprehension

Learn ⊙ **Skill Sequence**

- Sequence is the order in which things happen in a story.

- As you read, pay attention to what happens first, next, and last.

- A time line like the one below can help you keep track of the sequence.

Practice Read "Nalukataq, the Blanket Toss" on page 87. Look for clue words that help you understand the sequence.

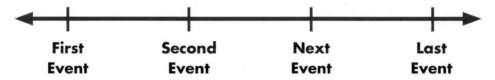

| First Event | Second Event | Next Event | Last Event |

On Your Own **Write to Read** Reread "Nalukataq, the Blanket Toss." Make a time line like the one above. Then use the time line to write a short paragraph describing the sequence of the blanket toss.

 Need a Review?
See *Picture It!*, p. PI•14 for more information about sequence.

 Ready to Try It?
As you read *Kumak's Fish*, pp. 88–103, look for events that happen first, next, and last.

G1R2.1 Identify text that uses sequence or other logical order.

NALUKATAQ, THE BLANKET TOSS

It is the end of June in Wainwright, Alaska. The whole village has come together for *Nalukataq*. This is the celebration of a good whale-hunting season. Whale is an important part of the people's diet. The people are glad that the whaling crew has returned.

The event begins with visiting. Then people get frozen whale meat. There is also a big feast. Then there are games, followed by music and dancing that go late into the night. One of the games is the blanket toss. In fact, the celebration is named for this event.

The nalukataq is a large round blanket made from walrus or seal skins. It has heavy rope handles for people to hold. First, about 15 people come together around the blanket. They lift it up. Then a person stands in the middle. The people holding the blanket toss and catch the person. The first jumper is always the captain of the crew that killed the whale.

The tradition comes from long ago. The blanket toss was once used in hunting. While a hunter was high in the air, he could see into the distance to find whales.

Skill Here is the first thing that happens at the celebration. You could add this to a time line.

Skill Clue words in this paragraph help you understand how the blanket toss is done.

Living and Learning

87

Kumak's Fish

Author and Illustrator:
Michael Bania

Genre A **Tall Tale** is a story that uses exaggeration. What is exaggerated in this story?

What happens when Kumak and his family go fishing?

89

On a beautiful Arctic morning Kumak looked out the window of his house. Through the willows he could see the sun rising over the frozen river.

"Ahhh, spring," said Kumak to his family.

"The days are long. The nights are short, and the ice is still hard. *Good day for fish.*"

"*Good day for fish*," said Kumak's wife, pulling on her warm parka.

"*Good day for fish*," said his wife's mother, pulling on her warm mukluks.

"*Good day for fish*," said his sons and daughters, pulling on their warm beaver hats and fur-lined gloves.

Kumak packed his fishing gear on his sled. He packed his wife on the sled. He packed his wife's mother on the sled. He packed his sons and daughters on the sled. And then, in the safest place of all, Kumak packed his Uncle Aglu's amazing hooking stick.

Everyone in the village knew of Uncle Aglu's amazing hooking stick. Uncle Aglu had carved it many years ago out of a piece of fine willow, and each spring he caught more fish than anyone in the village.

But this spring, Uncle Aglu's legs were stiff. He told Kumak to use the amazing hooking stick.

This was Kumak's lucky day!

When they reached the great, frozen lake past the mouth of the river, Kumak's family dug their fishing holes and sat down to wait.

Kumak and his family sat for a long time. They were quiet. They were patient. They scooped away the ice growing around their fishing holes.

Just as the sun was starting to turn down for the day, Kumak's oldest son caught a fish. Then Kumak's two daughters each caught a fish.

Soon his wife and his wife's mother each caught a fish. *"Good day for fish!"* they said.

Kumak was quiet. He was patient. He scooped away the ice growing around his fishing hole.

Suddenly, Uncle Aglu's amazing hooking stick began to twitch. It twitched this way. It twitched that way.

It went around and around.

It gave one more twitch, then yanked Kumak toward the fishing hole. "What a big fish!" said Kumak's wife. "Biggest I can remember!" said his wife's mother. "The biggest fish ever!" said his sons and daughters.

They danced with joy, thinking about the happy
faces of the villagers when they brought the fish home.
Just then, Kumak began to twitch.

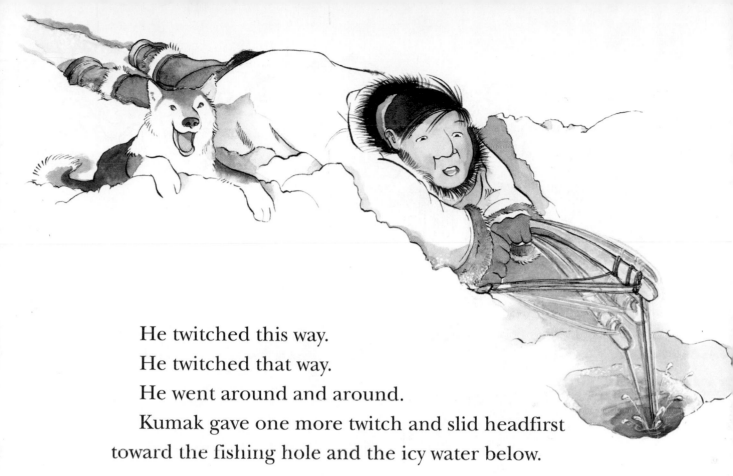

He twitched this way.

He twitched that way.

He went around and around.

Kumak gave one more twitch and slid headfirst toward the fishing hole and the icy water below.

"Wife! Help me pull this fish!"

Kumak's wife grabbed him around the waist and together they took two steps back.

"That fish must be as big as a seal!" yelled Kumak happily.

"Aana! Help me pull this fish!" His wife's
mother ran to help. She took hold of Kumak's wife
and together they took three steps back. "That fish
must be as big as a walrus!" yelled Kumak happily.

"Children! Help me pull this fish!" His sons and
daughters ran to help. They lined up, one behind the
other, and never let go. Together they took six more
steps, but the stick pulled them all the way back to the
edge of the hole.

"That fish must be as big as a whale!" yelled Kumak happily. Villagers on their way home heard Kumak's shouts and ran to help. They lined up behind Kumak's family and holding on tight to the person in front of them, they pulled and pulled. But no matter how many steps they took away from the hole, they always ended up back where they started.

Soon the whole village heard about Kumak's fish and came to help. In one long line stretching across the frozen lake, they pulled and pulled and **PULLED!**

Once again, Uncle Aglu's amazing hooking stick began to twitch. It twitched this way, and all the people of the village twitched this way.

It twitched that way, and all the people of the village twitched that way.

It went around and around, and all the people of the village went around and around.

Uncle Aglu's amazing hooking stick gave one more enormous twitch and pulled Kumak down the fishing hole and into the icy water below!

Kumak's family and the villagers didn't give up. Each person held on tight to the person in front of them and never let go. All together, they gave one more mighty pull and …

WHOOSH!

Kumak came flying back out of the fishing hole. Uncle Aglu's amazing hooking stick came flying out with him.

Stretched out in one long line, all around Kumak and the fishing hole, were hundreds of fish! Each fish held on tight to the one in front of it and never let go. Kumak had landed enough fish for the entire village to have a splendid feast.

"Hooray for Kumak!" cheered the villagers as they picked up the fish. "Hooray for Uncle Aglu's amazing hooking stick!" said Kumak as they started home.

It was a good day for fish.

Think, Talk and Write

Talk About It Kumak, his family, and his neighbors had to work together and keep trying to reach their goal. Tell about a time when you had to keep trying to get results.

1. Use the pictures below to retell the story. **Retell**

2. Create two time lines. On one, show the order in which Kumak's family caught their fish. On the other, show the order in which people lined up behind Kumak to help him pull the fish. **Sequence**

3. As you read, what questions did you ask yourself? How did they help you understand what you were reading? **Ask Questions**

4. The words *twitch* and *yanked* are strong action verbs. What other examples of strong verbs can you find in *Kumak's Fish?* **Vocabulary**

TEST PRACTICE

Look Back and Write Look back at the question on page 89. Think about the most important events that happened in the story. Now write a response to the question. Be sure to include details from the story to support your answer.

Meet author **and illustrator Michael Bania on page 447.**

Retell

   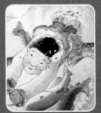  

R2.2 Ask questions and support answers by connecting prior knowledge with literal information found in, and inferred from, the text.

Writing

Prompt *Kumak's Fish* is a tall tale about a man who takes his family fishing. Think about an activity you'd like to do with your family. Now write a tall tale about that activity.

Writing Trait

Good **word choice** helps readers picture what is happening in the story.

Student Model

A Perfect Day

The sun is shining in the blue sky. A cool breeze keeps me from getting too hot. Today is a perfect day for canoeing! I am paddling down the river with my mom and dad and my brother Luke.

As we float along, we see a family of turtles sunning themselves on a log. Suddenly the sun disappears behind a huge cloud! We don't want clouds to ruin our beautiful day. What could we possibly do? So I take a deep breath and blow as hard as I can. Luke joins in. Together we keep blowing and blowing until the cloud begins to move! Soon it is sunny again.

Later, a few more clouds try to cover the sun. Each time, Luke and I fill our lungs and blow them away. Then we relax in the sunshine and enjoy the cool breeze. It's a perfect day for canoeing.

The writer chooses action verbs that show readers what is happening.

An interrogative sentence asks a question and ends with a question mark.

A tall tale tells about exaggerated people and actions.

Use the model to help you write your own tall tale.

Living and Learning

W2.1.b Write narratives: Include well-chosen details to develop the plot. **LC1.2** Identify subjects and verbs that are in agreement and identify and use pronouns, adjectives, compound words, and articles correctly in writing and speaking.

Skill Talk

Steps in a Process is one kind of text structure. Authors often use steps in a process when explaining how to make or do something. Numbered steps can show you how to do something.

▶ **Ready to Try It?**
Read "How to Catch a Fish." Look for numbered steps that tell the order in which the actions should be done.

Social Studies Link

This article says there are rules about the fish you catch in public lakes and rivers. Think about public lakes, rivers, or parks in your area. Use the library or the Internet to learn about the rules in one of these places. Think about why these rules are important and then report your findings to your class.

THE MIDGEVILLE TIMES

Kids' Corner

How to Catch a Fish

Vicki Edwards nearly broke the standing record for the largest fish caught in Lake Buchanan. Vicki follows a simple guide to catch her fish and she wanted to share it with our readers.

Step 1. Bait the hook.
Have an adult help you bait your hook. There are different kinds of bait to choose from. Knowing what kind of fish you are trying to catch will help you decide which bait to use.

Step 2. Cast your line.

After you cast your line, watch the water. Ripples or small waves may indicate that fish are near. It is important to be quiet so you won't scare the fish away.

Step 3. Reel the fish in.

If your line tugs, that may mean you have a fish. Reel it in quickly so your fish cannot get loose. If the fish is very heavy, you may need a net to help you get your fish into the boat.

Step 4. See your prize.

Most lakes and rivers have rules and regulations that tell you if a fish is large enough for you to keep. Be sure to check those rules before you go fishing. Whether or not your fish is large enough to keep, be sure to take a photo of it!

Reading Across Texts

How is the method of fishing described here like Kumak's way of fishing? How is it different? Make a Venn diagram to compare and contrast the two methods of fishing.

Writing Across Texts Write a short paragraph contrasting Vicki Edwards's way of fishing with Kumak's method.

Let's Talk About
Wants and Needs

LS1.7 Use clear and specific vocabulary to communicate ideas and establish the tone.

Living and Learning

Build Vocabulary

Learn ⦿ **Skill Homographs** are words that are spelled the same but have different meanings. For example, *store* can be a noun meaning "a place to buy things." *Store* is also a verb that means "to put something away." Sometimes homographs have different sounds, such as *PROduce* (fruits and vegetables) and *proDUCE* (to make). When you see a word you know but the meaning doesn't make sense, it may be a homograph. Context clues, or the nearby words and sentences, can help you find the correct meaning of a homograph.

Practice Read "The Library" on page 111. Look for words that might be homographs. Read the nearby words and sentences for context clues.

Words to Know	laundry	shelves	variety
	spoiled	store	section
	traded	thousands	

On Your Own Reread "The Library." Make a list of the homographs you find. Then write both meanings of each word. If you need help, use your glossary or a dictionary.

R1.4 Use knowledge of antonyms, synonyms, homophones, and homographs to determine the meanings of words. **R1.6** Use sentence and word context to find the meaning of unknown words.

The Library

Martita was cleaning her room. She picked up her dirty clothes and put them into the basket with the other laundry. "Let's finish our chores," her mother said. "We'll go to the library as soon as you're done."

Now Martita was eager to finish. She put her books on the shelves. Under the bed she found a variety of puzzle pieces and magazines. In the kitchen, Martita washed the dishes left from breakfast. Then she put the milk away so that it would not get spoiled. "I'm done!" she called to her mother. "Let's go!"

They stopped at the grocery store first. Martita chose the vegetables they'd cook for dinner that night.

"You've been helping so much with the chores," her mother said. "Today you can check out two books from the library instead of one."

This made Martita feel proud. At the library, she headed for the children's section. She picked a book and read the back cover. Then she traded it for another one. There were thousands of books to choose from! But she finally chose the two she wanted. "If I clean my room every day, can I check out three books next time?" she asked her mother.

 Need a Review?
See *Words!*, p. W•10 for more information about homographs.

▶ **Ready to Try It?**
Read *Supermarket*, pp. 114–133.

Living and Learning

Build Comprehension

Learn ⊙ **Skill Steps in a Process**

- When you read about the order in which something happens, you are following the steps in a process.

- Instructions for making or doing something are also steps in a process.

- Clue words such as *first*, *second*, and *next* can help you keep the steps in order. Sometimes the steps are numbered.

- If there are no clue words or numbers, use your common sense and what you already know about the process to put the steps in order in your mind.

Practice   Read "A Breakfast Treat" on page 113. Look for clue words that help you understand the steps in a process.

On Your Own   **Write to Read** Reread "A Breakfast Treat." As you read each step, think about how the result will look. Then write the steps in a numbered list.

 Need a Review?
See *Picture It!*, p. PI•15 for more information about steps in a process.

 Ready to Try It?
Read *Supermarket*, pp. 114–133. Look for steps in a process that the author has described for you.

R2.7 Follow simple multiple-set written instructions (e.g., how to assemble a product or play a board game).

A Breakfast Treat

Are you ready for a changed breakfast time? Try French toast. It is easy to make. You only need a few ingredients: three eggs, three tablespoons of milk, some butter, and six slices of bread. Before you begin, ask an adult to help you.

Skill Here is a clue word—*Before*. The writer tells you that asking an adult is the first thing to do.

To start, crack the eggs into a big bowl. Pour in the milk. Mix with a whisk or a fork. You can also add a bit of vanilla or cinnamon if you like.

Next, put a frying pan over medium heat. Wait a minute or two, and then check to see if the pan is hot enough. Sprinkle a few drops of water in it. If they dance and sizzle, the pan is ready. Then melt a little butter in the pan.

Dip a bread slice into the egg mixture. Make sure it gets completely covered. Carefully place two bread slices in the pan. Cook for about two minutes until they start to brown. Then flip them over. Cook for another minute or so. Repeat with the rest of the bread. Serve hot with more butter and maple syrup. Yum!

Skill There are no clue words here, but you can use your common sense. These steps need to be done in the order in which they are written.

Genre

Narrative Nonfiction gives facts about real people and places in the form of a story. Look for interesting facts about supermarkets.

Supermarket

Author: Kathleen Krull

Illustrator: Melanie Hope Greenberg

How does food get to our supermarkets?

Shopping carts clang.
Magic doors whiz open and shut.
Colors glow under bright white lights.
So many breakfasts, lunches, and dinners!
It's all at a special, necessary, very real place:
the supermarket.

The supermarket is a whole world of its own. Where does all this crunchy, munchy, sweet, sour, fiery, frozen, fabulous food come from?

The doors don't really open by magic. When an electric "eye" overhead "sees" you coming, it starts a motor to open the doors.

It all begins on farms.

Our food comes from places with lots of sunshine, rich soil, and clean water.

Certain states are famous for certain foods. Iowa for popcorn, Vermont for maple syrup, Michigan for cereal, Wisconsin for cheese, Idaho for potatoes, Massachusetts for cranberries, Florida for oranges, California for grapes, Georgia for peaches and peanuts.

Farmers make decisions every day during the long
months of growing.

At harvesttime, workers pick the fruits and vegetables.

They pack everything neatly in boxes and load the
boxes onto trucks.

Picking fruits and vegetables can be
painful, low-paying work. César Chavez
(1927-1993) became a hero for
workers when he founded the National
Farm Workers of America.

Small trucks, big trucks, gigantic trucks— all rev up their engines.

Every night, drivers take off from farms or warehouses. They zoom down the highway toward your town.

Among many other foods, American Indians introduced to the rest of the world chocolate, potatoes, tomatoes, beans, peppers, and most important, corn. Some form of corn appears in more supermarket foods today than probably anything else.

In early America, most people were farmers. American Indians taught the new arrivals what to grow.

Families grew all their own food.

Later they traded food with one another to get other things they needed.

They started using money to buy things at town marketplaces.

Soon there were general stores where you could buy
almost anything and little, family-run grocery stores—
"mom-and-pop" stores. Stores became bigger, dividing
items into different departments.

Now we have an amazing place where every morning workers have a whole "super" market all ready for you.

They have unpacked thousands of boxes and arranged everything on the shelves, just so.

Bananas are the most popular fruit, followed by apples, watermelons, oranges, cantaloupes, grapes, grapefruits, strawberries, peaches, and pears.

You can find more variety in the fruit and vegetable section than anywhere else: fresh, juicy, strange, familiar.

Shoppers look, touch, sniff, compare, weigh— and watch out for automatic sprayers.

Beds of crushed ice keep the meats and fish fresh. Butchers cut or grind meat into different sizes and wrap packages in plastic.

For most of human history, food has often spoiled before it could be eaten. Not until the 1800s did people learn how to preserve food by sealing it inside metal cans. Around 1830, the English figured out a way to chill their food with machines.

According to surveys, the top reasons why shoppers pick a particular store are:
1. location
2. prices, and
3. selection

The best smells float around the bakery.
Bakers sometimes bake thousands of doughnuts
a day and at least a dozen different kinds of bread.

Just about everyone stops in the dairy section. Behind all the eggs, milk, yogurt, and cheese is a refrigerated area keeping everything cold.

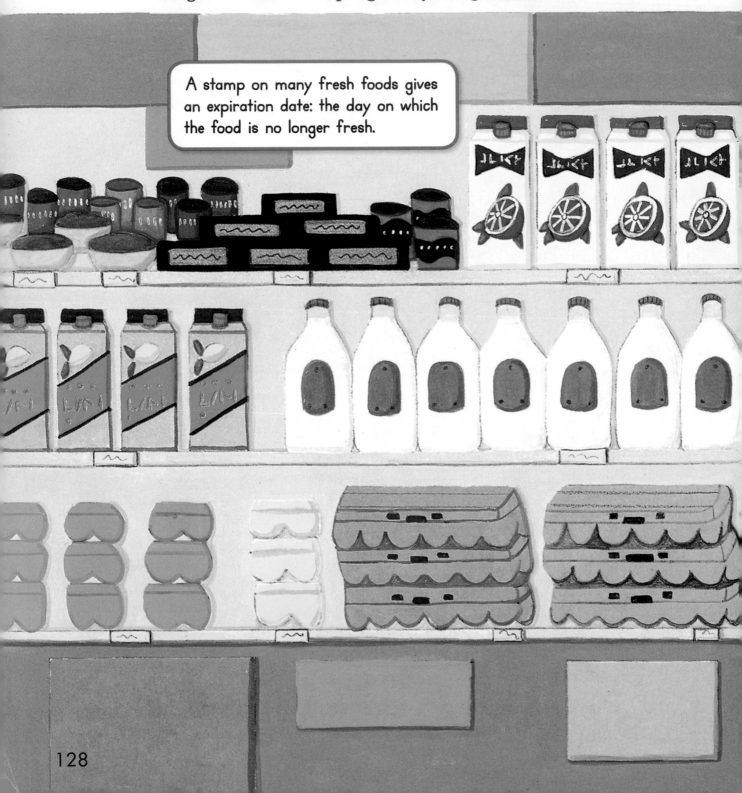

A stamp on many fresh foods gives an expiration date: the day on which the food is no longer fresh.

A sweater is handy in the frozen foods section, where the air is coldest. Zippy music makes some people hum along or dance right in the aisle.

129

The store is packed with cereal, soups, spices, and even "nonfoods."

What is a "nonfood"? Something in a supermarket that we don't eat—like toilet paper, laundry soap, toothpaste, shampoo, and magazines.

At the checkout counter, people try to pick the shortest line.

An electronic scanner "reads" the bar codes on most products and prints out the prices. A cash register adds up the cost of your food. Baggers ask "Paper or plastic?" and pack up your groceries.

Think about all the people who move food from the farms to your kitchen shelves!

The average wait in the checkout line is 8 minutes.

Americans spend more than $440 BILLION a year at our supermarkets.

Over half of shoppers, especially women, use a shopping list to make sure they don't forget anything. The average shopping list contains 22 items. Still, over half of what shoppers buy in a store is not on their list.

The supermarket is never quite the same from day to day. New items are added all the time, especially from around the world. Some markets have other stores right inside—worlds of their own.

Think, Talk and Write

Talk About It You probably already knew some things about supermarkets before you read this selection. How did your prior knowledge help you to understand what you were reading?

1. Use the pictures below to summarize what you learned. **Summarize**

2. *Supermarket* explains how fruits and vegetables get from the farms to the store shelves. List the steps in order. **Steps in a Process**

3. As you read this selection, were there any places where you became confused? What fix-up strategies did you use? **Monitor and Clarify**

4. A supermarket is organized into *sections*. What are some other things that have sections? **Vocabulary**

TEST PRACTICE

Look Back and Write Look back at the question on page 115. Think about all the different people who help get food to the supermarket. Now write a paragraph about the job of one of those people. Use details from the selection in your answer.

Meet author **Kathleen Krull on page 448.**

Summarize

G2R2.5 Restate facts and details in the text to clarify and organize ideas.

Writing

Prompt *Supermarket* is a real story that tells how a supermarket works. Think about a time when you had to go to a store to get something you needed. Now write a real description of the store.

Writing Trait

Voice shows a writer's style and personality.

Student Model

Harry's Hardware

For such a small place, Harry's Hardware sure sells many things. Cleaning supplies sit next to hoses, buckets, and watering cans. Boards of different sizes lean against the counter.

One row has lots of little boxes full of nails, screws, and other bits and pieces. Harry counts them out for his customers. He puts them in small paper bags. Next to the boxes, hammers and saws hang on hooks.

In one corner, there's a rack of cards showing all the different paint colors you can buy. Harry can mix the paint right there in the store! A loud machine shakes the paint can very fast to mix up the colors.

A lively voice keeps readers interested.

Adjectives create a picture of the store.

Exclamatory sentences show strong feelings.

Use the model to help you write your own description.

W2.2 Write descriptions that use concrete sensory details to present and support unified impressions of people, places, things, or experiences.

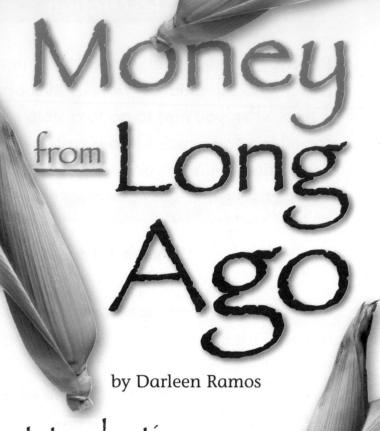

Money from Long Ago

by Darleen Ramos

Introduction

In ancient times, people did not use paper money or coins. They traded to get things they needed. A person might trade three ears of corn for five potatoes. A farmer might trade a sheep for several chickens.

If the trade was not even, people used other things for payment. They may have used beans, shells, furs, or tools. Here are a few items people used as money.

Cowrie Shells

Cowries are small snails that live in the ocean. In ancient times, their shiny shells were used as money in China, India, and parts of Africa. The shells are one of the oldest forms of payment. Cowrie shells could be stored or worn. The color and size of the shell would set its price.

Cowrie shells

Feather Coils

Before there were coins and paper money, the people on the Pacific island of Santa Cruz used a feather coil for money. The coil was made from the red feathers of a honey-eating bird. The feathers were glued on the coil, which is about ten yards long. Red feather money was used in marriage contracts and to buy boats.

Red feather money coil

Salt Bar

Hundreds of years ago, people from Africa and China used salt as money. Pure salt was expensive. Salt was used to keep food from going bad. The salt was cut into standard sizes and covered in reeds. This protected the salt from breaking. It also kept people from scratching off some of the salt between trades.

Reed protecting a salt bar

Stone Discs

Long ago, the people from Yap, an island in the Pacific, used large stone discs as money. The stones had holes in the middle. The giant discs were not moved when paid to a new owner. That's because the largest stones weighed over 400 pounds! People used the stone discs to arrange marriages and to trade houses or boats.

Stone disc

Wampum

Centuries ago, Native Americans used a belt of beads for trading. This wampum was made from clam shells that were smoothed into beads. Each belt was special. The bead maker used different colors and patterns. Wampum belts were also traded during peace agreements.

Wampum belt

Reading Across Texts

If you were going shopping at a supermarket, would you rather use today's paper money and coins, or the kinds of money people used long ago? Why?

Writing Across Texts Make a chart. List the "good" and the "bad" of each kind of money.

Let's Talk About
Saving and Spending

LS1.7 Use clear and specific vocabulary to communicate ideas and establish the tone.

Fresh
Lemonade

141

Build Vocabulary

Learn ◉ **Skill Prefixes and Suffixes** When you see a word you don't know, look closely at the word. Does it have a prefix at the beginning? A prefix is a word part added in front of a base word to form a new word. Does it have a suffix at the end? A suffix is a word part added to the end of a base word to form a new word. You can use prefixes and suffixes to figure out the meaning of the word.

> The prefix *un-* makes a word mean "not _____" or "the opposite of _____." For example, *unhappy* means "not happy."

> The suffix *-ly* makes a word mean "in a _____ way." For example, *slowly* means "in a slow way."

Practice Read "A Gift for Cletus" on page 143. As you read, study the highlighted words. Decide which ones have a prefix or a suffix. Make a list of the words with prefixes or suffixes.

Words to Know	errands	bundles	steady
	wobbled	dangerously	arranged
	unwrapped	excitedly	

On Your Own Reread "A Gift for Cletus." Find the word *steady* in the first paragraph and write it down. This is your base word. Now add a prefix to make a word that means "not steady." Use the new word in a sentence about Cletus and his bike.

R1.8 Use knowledge of prefixes (e.g., *un-, re-, pre-, bi-, mis-, dis-*) and suffixes (e.g., *-er, -est, -ful*) to determine the meaning of words.

A GIFT FOR CLETUS

Every Saturday Cletus ran **errands** for his neighbors to earn money. They gave him lists of things to buy in town. They gave him **bundles** to drop off. Sometimes Cletus had so much piled on the front of his bike that he could not keep the bike **steady**. He **wobbled dangerously** from side to side, and the bundles would almost fall into the street. Cletus had to ride very slowly, keeping one hand on the bundles.

Cletus wanted to buy a big basket for the back of his bike. He knew that with the bundles arranged behind him, it would be easier and **safer** to ride back and forth to town. But he had not saved enough money yet.

The neighbors really **appreciated** what Cletus did for them. They wanted a way to say *thank you*. So they all got together and bought Cletus a basket for his bike. He **unwrapped** the gift and **excitedly** put the new basket on his bike. He thanked his neighbors, and then off he went again with their lists and bundles.

 Need a Review?
See *Words!*, pp. W•5–W•6 for more information about prefixes and suffixes.

▶ **Ready to Try It?**
Read *My Rows and Piles of Coins*, pp. 146–160.

Build Comprehension

Learn ⊙ **Skill Character and Setting**

- Characters are the people or animals in a story. Setting is the time and place in which a story happens.

- If the author does not directly describe a character, look for clues in the character's words, thoughts, and actions.

- An author may tell you the setting, or you may figure it out from details in the story.

- Sometimes you can use what you've figured out about a character to predict what they will do next in the story.

Practice Read "Saturday Is Market Day" on page 145. Think about where and when the story takes place. Also look for clues about the characters.

Story Title	
Characters	Setting

On Your Own **Write to Read** Reread "Saturday Is Market Day." Think about the girl telling the story. Use what you've figured out about her to write a paragraph predicting what she will do next.

 Need a Review?
See *Picture It!*, p. PI•12 for more information about character and setting.

▷ **Ready to Try It?**
As you read *My Rows and Piles of Coins*, pp. 146–160, watch for details that help you understand the characters and setting.

144   **G1R3.1** Identify and describe the elements of plot, setting, and character(s) in a story, as well as the story's beginning, middle, and ending.

Saturday Is Market Day

We got up before the sun to make the trip into town. My family lives in a little village in Africa. Every Saturday we go to town to sell our head scarves. Mama makes the scarves. Sometimes I help. They are the very best scarves you could buy.

Papa pulled the cart into the market as the sun came up. My sister Fusi and I laid out the scarves. We ate breakfast before our first customer came.

It was not long before we sold our first scarves. A woman and her daughter bought them. Soon we began to sell many more.

At ten, drummers set up near us. As they played, Papa and Fusi danced. Mama and I clapped along.

In the afternoon, one customer had me turn around and around. She was looking at the scarf I was wearing. I had made it myself. She bought my scarf!

It was a good market day. I am looking forward to next Saturday.

Skill This is a good place to stop and think about the characters and the setting. The story takes place in a village in Africa, and the main character is a child who helps her family sell scarves.

Skill This paragraph gives a clue about the character—she feels proud when a customer buys the scarf she had made herself.

Living and Learing

145

MY ROWS AND PILES OF COINS

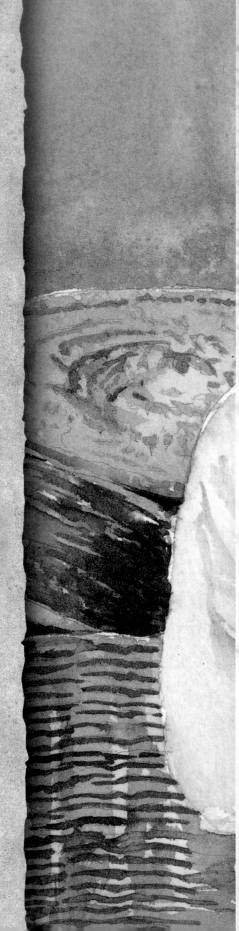

by Tololwa M. Mollel

illustrated by E. B. Lewis

Why does the boy put his coins into piles and rows?

After a good day at the market, my mother, Yeyo, gave me five whole ten-cent coins. I gaped at the money until Yeyo nudged me. "Saruni, what are you waiting for? Go and buy yourself something."

I plunged into the market. I saw roasted peanuts, *chapati,* rice cakes, and *sambusa.* There were wooden toy trucks, kites, slingshots, and marbles. My heart beat excitedly. I wanted to buy everything, but I clutched my coins tightly in my pocket.

At the edge of the market, I stopped. In a neat sparkling row stood several big new bicycles. One of them was decorated all over with red and blue.

That's what I would buy!

For some time now, Murete, my father, had been teaching me to ride his big, heavy bicycle. If only I had a bicycle of my own!

A gruff voice startled me. "What are you looking for, little boy?"

I turned and bumped into a tall skinny man, who laughed at my confusion. Embarrassed, I hurried back to Yeyo.

That night, I dropped five ten-cent coins into my
secret money box. It held other ten-cent coins Yeyo had
given me for helping with market work on Saturdays.
By the dim light of a lantern, I feasted my eyes on the
money. I couldn't believe it was all mine.

I emptied the box, arranged all the coins in piles
and the piles in rows. Then I counted the coins and
thought about the bicycle I longed to buy.

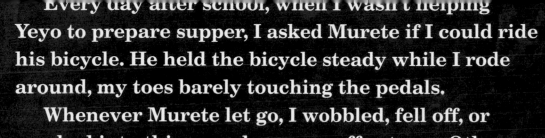

Every day after school, when I wasn't helping
Yeyo to prepare supper, I asked Murete if I could ride
his bicycle. He held the bicycle steady while I rode
around, my toes barely touching the pedals.

Whenever Murete let go, I wobbled, fell off, or
crashed into things and among coffee trees. Other
children from the neighborhood had a good laugh
watching me.

Go on, laugh, I thought, sore but determined.
Soon I would be like a cheetah on wheels, racing on
errands with my very own bicycle!

Saturday after Saturday, we took goods to market, piled high on Yeyo's head and on my squeaky old wooden wheelbarrow. We sold dried beans and maize, pumpkins, spinach, bananas, firewood, and eggs.

My money box grew heavier.

I emptied the box, arranged the coins in piles and the piles in rows. Then I counted the coins and thought about the blue and red bicycle.

After several more lessons Murete let me ride on my own while he shouted instructions. *"Eyes up, arms straight, keep pedaling, slow down!"* I enjoyed the breeze on my face, the pedals turning smoothly under my feet, and, most of all, Yeyo's proud smile as she watched me ride. How surprised she would be to see my new bicycle! And how grateful she would be when I used it to help her on market days!

The heavy March rains came. The ground became so muddy, nobody went to market. Instead, I helped Yeyo with house chores. When it wasn't raining, I helped Murete on the coffee farm. We pruned the coffee trees and put fallen leaves and twigs around the coffee stems. Whenever I could, I practiced riding Murete's bicycle.

It stopped raining in June. Not long after, school closed. Our harvest—fresh maize and peas, sweet potatoes, vegetables, and fruits—was so big, we went to market on Saturdays *and* Wednesdays. My money box grew heavier and heavier.

I emptied the box, arranged the coins in piles and the piles in rows. Then I counted the coins and thought about the bicycle I would buy.

A few days later I grew confident enough to try to ride a loaded bicycle. With Murete's help, I strapped a giant pumpkin on the carrier behind me. When I attempted to pedal, the bicycle wobbled so dangerously that Murete, alongside me, had to grab it.

"All right, Saruni, the load is too heavy for you," he said, and I got off. Mounting the bicycle to ride back to the house, he sighed wearily. "And hard on my bones, which are getting too old for pedaling."

I practiced daily with smaller loads, and slowly I learned to ride a loaded bicycle. No more pushing the squeaky old wheelbarrow, I thought. I would ride with my load tall and proud on my bicycle—just like Murete!

On the first Saturday after school opened in July, we went to market as usual. Late in the afternoon, after selling all we had, Yeyo sat talking with another trader.

I set off into the crowd. I wore an old coat Murete had handed down to me for chilly July days like today. My precious coins were wrapped in various bundles inside the oversize pockets of the coat.

I must be the richest boy in the world, I thought, feeling like a king. *I can buy anything.*

The tall skinny man was polishing his bicycles as I came up. "I want to buy a bicycle," I said, and brought out my bundles of coins.

The man whistled in wonder as I unwrapped the money carefully on his table. "How many coins have you got there?"

Proudly, I told him. "Three hundred and five."

"Three hundred and . . . five," he muttered. "Mmh, that's . . . thirty shillings and fifty cents." He exploded with laughter. "A whole bicycle . . . for thirty shillings . . . and fifty cents?"

His laugh followed me as I walked away with my bundles of coins, deeply disappointed.

On our way home, Yeyo asked what was wrong.
I had to tell her everything.

"You saved all your money for a bicycle to help me?"
she asked. I could tell she was amazed and touched.
"How nice of you!" As for the tall skinny man, she
scoffed, "*Oi!* What does he know? Of course you will
buy a bicycle. One day you will."

Her kind words did not cheer me.

The next afternoon, the sound of a
pikipiki filled the air, *tuk-tuk-tuk-tuk-tuk.*
I came out of the house and stared in
astonishment. Murete was perched on
an orange motorbike.

He cut the engine and dismounted. Then,
chuckling at my excited questions about the
pikipiki, he headed into the house.

When Murete came out, Yeyo was with him, and
he was wheeling his bicycle. "I want to sell this to you.
For thirty shillings and fifty cents." He winked at me.

Surprised, I stared at Murete. How did he know
about my secret money box? I hadn't told him anything.

Then suddenly, I realized the wonderful thing
that had just happened. "My bicycle, I have my very
own bicycle!" I said, and it didn't matter at all that it
wasn't decorated with red and blue. Within moments,
I had brought Murete my money box.

158

Murete gave Yeyo the box. Yeyo, in turn, gave it to me. Puzzled, I looked from Yeyo to Murete and to Yeyo again. "You're giving it . . . back to me?"

Yeyo smiled. "It's a reward for all your help to us."

"Thank you, thank you!" I cried gleefully.

The next Saturday, my load sat tall and proud on my bicycle, which I walked importantly to market. I wasn't riding it because Yeyo could never have kept up.

Looking over at Yeyo, I wished she didn't have to carry such a big load on her head.

If only I had a cart to pull behind my bicycle, I thought, *I could lighten her load!*

That night I emptied the box, arranged all the coins in piles and the piles in rows. Then I counted the coins and thought about the cart I would buy. . . .

Think, Talk and Write

Talk About It What does Saruni want at the start of the story? What does he want at the end? What happens during the story to cause this change?

1. Use the pictures below to retell the story. **Retell**

2. How would you describe Saruni? **Character**

3. What problem did Saruni have at the beginning of the story? How was his problem resolved at the end? **Story Structure**

4. Use words from the Words to Know list to write an e-mail to a friend telling a funny story about Saruni and his bicycle. **Vocabulary**

TEST PRACTICE

Look Back and Write Look back at the question on page 147. Also look at pages 150–154. Now write a response to the question. Be sure to include details from the story to support your answer.

Meet author **Tololwa Mollel on page 449** and illustrator **E. B. Lewis on page 449.**

Retell

  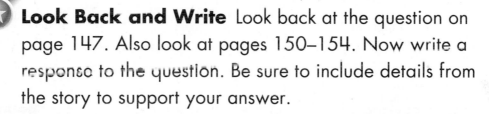    

 R3.3 Determine what characters are like by what they say or do and by how the author or illustrator portrays them.

Writing

Realistic Story

Prompt In *My Rows and Piles of Coins*, a boy saves his money for a special purchase. Think about something you would like to buy. Now write a realistic story about how you would save for it.

Writing Trait

Using different kinds of **sentences** makes writing lively and interesting.

Student Model

Earning Money

I want to buy my little sister a tea set for her birthday. My dad says it costs $15. My sister's birthday is only a week away! How will I earn the money?

First I ask Mom and Dad if I can do some extra chores. "Great idea!" Mom says. Dad makes me a list.

1. Clean up the basement.
2. Pull the weeds in the garden.
3. Wash the car.

They agree to pay me $10 if I do everything on the list by Sunday. Then I will need only $5 more!

I go next door and offer to walk Mrs. Peterson's dog after school. I explain why I'm trying to earn money. Mrs. Peterson says she would be happy to pay me fifty cents each time I walk Skipper, and then she has another idea. "I'll pay you $3 to help me give Skipper a bath tomorrow," she says.

Now I know I can earn enough for my sister's gift.

Exclamations make your writing sound natural.

Compound sentences combine two sentences together.

Story events could happen in real life.

Use the model to help you write your own realistic story.

162 **W2.1.b** Write narratives: Include well-chosen details to develop the plot.

Hints for Writing Sentences

- Use different words to start your sentences. Starting too many sentences with *I, he, she, the,* or *a* can be boring.

- Perk up your writing by adding questions, commands, and exclamations.

- Vary the lengths of sentences.

- Avoid writing long, stringy sentences.

- Short, choppy sentences sometimes can be combined with connecting words.

LC1.1 Understand and be able to use complete and correct declarative, interrogative, imperative, and exclamatory sentences in writing and speaking.

163

Living and Learning

Web Sites are found on the Internet. Each Web site has an address also called a URL, that usually begins with *http://*. The home page introduces the Web site and works like a table of contents. *Links* are words on the Web site that appear in color or underlined.

 Ready to Try It?
Read "Learning About Money." Use the illustrations and captions to learn how to read a Web site.

Social Studies Link

List ways you could earn money. Think about how long it might take to save for something you want to buy. Then write about what you would do with your earnings.

Learning About Money

In *My Rows and Piles of Coins,* Saruni saves his money for a new bicycle. This story may have made you wonder how young people can learn about money. After searching the Internet, you might find a Web site that helps kids learn about money.

for more practice

Get Online!

PearsonSuccessNet.com

A Money Web Site

**Want to save money and make it grow?
Click on a link and find out how.**

Let's say you need a plan, so you click here.

If you click on Save as You Spend, you might see the following.

If you click on Tip 1 <u>Set a Goal</u>, you will find this information.

Money Web Site

Set a Goal

Suppose your goal is a new pair of sneakers that costs $48, and you earn $12 a week mowing lawns. What's your plan? How quickly do you want those sneakers?

Plan 1 If you save $6 a week, it will take you eight weeks to save enough to buy them (6 × 8 = 48). Are you patient enough to wait nearly two months?

Plan 2 If you save $12 a week, you can buy the sneakers in only four weeks (4 × 12 = 48). That's twice as fast! But then you won't have any extra spending money during those four weeks. Which goal would you set? It's up to you.

Reading Across Texts
Which method of saving does Saruni follow in saving for a bike, Plan 1 or Plan 2?

Writing Across Texts In a letter to Saruni, explain the method he chose.

Solitude

by A. A. Milne

I have a house where I go
When there's too many people,
I have a house where I go
Where no one can be;
I have a house where I go,
Where nobody ever says "No";
Where no one says anything—so
There is no one but me.

The World's So Big

by Aileen Fisher

Think of all the people
I'll never get to know
Because the world's so big
And my wagon's so slow.

Think of all the places
I'll never get to see
Because the street's so long
And Mother's calling me!

Money

by Richard Armour

Workers earn it,
Spendthrifts burn it,
Bankers lend it,
Shoppers spend it,
Forgers fake it,
Taxes take it,
Dying leave it,
Heirs receive it,
Thrifty save it,
Misers crave it,
Robbers seize it,
Rich increase it,
Gamblers lose it . . .
I could use it.

Transportation

by Betsy Franco

Cars, trucks,
rockets, planes,
canoes, boats,
bikes, and trains.
Motorbikes, buses,
skateboards, feet,
subways, taxis,
trolleys in the street.
So many ways
to travel around:
in water, in air,
or down on the ground.
We'll fly to Mars
or rocket to the moon
in passenger spaceships
very, very soon.
We can drive or pedal
or walk or row.
Transportation takes us
wherever we go!

Smart Solutions

THE BIG ?

What are smart ways that problems are solved?

Penguin Chick EXPOSITORY NONFICTION

What plant and animal structures help solve problems?

Paired Selection
Plants: Fitting into Their World PHOTO ESSAY

First Day in Grapes REALISTIC FICTION

How do you know if a solution is a good solution?

Paired Selection
The Big Soccer Game E-MAIL

Prudy's Problem and How She Solved It FANTASY

When is it time to find a solution?

Paired Selection
Meeting the Challenge of Collecting INTERVIEW

Tops & Bottoms ANIMAL FANTASY

What can we do to make sure solutions are fair?

Paired Selection
The Hare and the Tortoise FABLE

Amazing Bird Nests EXPOSITORY NONFICTION

How have plants and animals adapted to solve problems?

Paired Selection
A Journey into Adaptation with Max Axiom, Super Scientist NARRATIVE NONFICTION

Smart Solutions

Let's Talk About
Plant and Animal Structures

LS1.7 Use clear and specific vocabulary to communicate ideas and establish the tone.

Build Vocabulary

Learn ⊙ **Skill Synonyms** When you are reading and you come to a word you don't know, read the nearby words and sentences. The author may give you a synonym for the word. A synonym is a word that has the same or almost the same meaning as another word. For example, *jump* and *leap* are synonyms. Look for a word that might be a synonym. It can help you understand the meaning of the word you don't know.

Practice Read "Penguins Are Birds" on page 177. As you read, look for synonyms to help you understand the meanings of the highlighted words. Make a list of the highlighted words and any synonyms you find.

Words to Know	hatch	pecks	snuggles
	preen	flippers	frozen
	cuddles		

On Your Own Reread "Penguins Are Birds." Now look at the pictures on pages 184–191. Choose a picture to write about. Write a short description of the picture using words from your list.

176 🐻 **R1.4** Use knowledge of antonyms, synonyms, homophones, and homographs to determine the meanings of words. **R1.6** Use sentence and word context to find the meaning of unknown words.

Penguins Are Birds

All birds come from eggs. The mother bird lays the eggs, and then the mother bird or the father bird sits on the eggs until it is time for them to hatch. Each baby bird pecks and hits the shell of its egg with its beak until the shell breaks open. The baby bird cannot fly or get food. It needs its parents to bring it food and keep it warm. When a parent bird sits on the nest, the baby bird snuggles, or presses, into the parent's belly. The parents preen their own feathers. Then they also brush the baby bird's soft feathers. This helps keep the baby bird warm.

Penguins are birds. They have flippers instead of wings, and they swim rather than fly. But they have feathers and lay eggs just as other birds do. Baby penguins hatch from eggs, and they need their parents to give them food and warmth. Some penguins live in Antarctica, where the land and much of the water around it are frozen. Penguins don't have nests, so a penguin parent cuddles, or hugs, the egg or the chick to keep it warm.

 Need a Review?
See *Words!*, p. W•3 for more information about synonyms.

 Ready to Try It?
Read *Penguin Chick*, pp. 180–193.

Build Comprehension

Learn ⊙ **Skill Main Idea and Details**

- The topic is what a piece of writing is all about.

- The main idea is the most important idea about the topic.

- Supporting details are small pieces of information that tell more about the main idea.

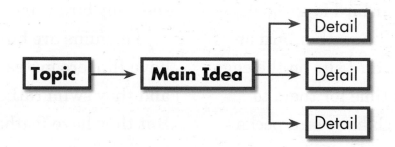

Practice Read "The Coldest Continent" on page 179. Make a graphic organizer like the one above to show the topic, the main idea, and three details of the first paragraph.

On Your Own **Write to Read** Reread "The Coldest Continent." Add two more "main idea" boxes to your graphic organizer, one to show the main idea of the second paragraph and one for the third paragraph. Then use the organizer to help you write a one-paragraph summary of "The Coldest Continent."

 Need a Review?
See *Picture It!*, p. PI•9 for more help with main idea and details.

 Ready to Try It?
As you read *Penguin Chick*, pp. 180–193, watch for details that help you understand the main idea.

  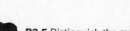 R2.5 Distinguish the main idea and supporting details in expository text.

The Coldest Continent

Antarctica is not like any other continent. It is as far south as you can go on Earth. The South Pole is found there. Ice covers the whole land. In some places the ice is almost three miles thick! Beneath the ice are mountains and valleys.

Skill You can see that the topic of this passage is Antarctica, but the main idea of the paragraph is that Antarctica is covered with ice.

The weather in Antarctica is harsh. It is the coldest place on Earth. The temperature does not get above freezing. It is also one of the windiest places in the world.

Not many living things are found in Antarctica. People go there to study for only a short time. Very few animals can live there. Yet many animals live on nearby islands. Seals and penguins swim in the ocean waters. They build nests on the land. Some birds spend their summers in Antarctica. But most of the continent is just ice, snow, and cold air.

Skill The last two sentences contain supporting details.

Penguin Chick

by Betty Tatham
illustrated by Helen K. Davie

Genre **Expository nonfiction** gives information about the real world. Read for facts about emperor penguins.

How do emperor penguins protect their chicks
from the extreme temperature of Antarctica?

A fierce wind howls. It whips snow across the ice. Here, a female emperor penguin has just laid an egg. It is the only egg she will lay this year.

Most birds build nests for their eggs. But on the ice in Antarctica, there are no twigs or leaves. There is no grass or mud. Nothing to build a nest with. Nothing but snow and ice.

The new penguin father uses his beak to scoop the egg onto his webbed feet.

He tucks it under his feather-covered skin, into a special place called a *brood patch*. The egg will be as snug and warm there as if it were in a sleeping bag.

One of the penguin parents must stay with the egg to keep it warm. But where penguins lay their eggs, there is no food for them to eat.

The penguin father is bigger and fatter than the mother. He can live longer without food. So the father penguin stays with the egg while the mother travels to the sea to find food.

The two parents sing together before the mother penguin leaves.

Along with many other penguins, the mother penguin leaves the rookery, where she laid her egg.

The mother walks or slides on her belly. This is called *tobogganing*. She uses her flippers and webbed feet to push herself forward over ice and snow.

Because it's winter in Antarctica, water near
the shore is frozen for many miles. After three days
the mother penguin comes to the end of the ice. She
dives into the water to hunt for fish, squid, and tiny
shrimplike creatures called *krill*.

Fish

Squid

Krill

Back at the rookery, the penguin fathers form a group called a *huddle*. They stand close together for warmth. Each keeps his own egg warm.

For two months the penguin father always keeps his egg on his feet. When he walks, he shuffles his feet so the egg doesn't roll away. He sleeps standing up. He has no food to eat, but the fat on his body keeps him alive.

Finally he feels the chick move inside the egg. The chick pecks and pecks and pecks. In about three days the egg cracks open.

The chick is wet. But soon his soft feathers, called *down,* dry and become fluffy and gray. The father still keeps the chick warm in the brood patch. Sometimes the chick pokes his head out. But while he's so little, he must stay covered. And he must stay on his father's feet. Otherwise the cold would kill him.

The father talks to the chick in his trumpet voice. The chick answers with a whistle.

The father's trumpet call echoes across the ice. The penguin mother is on her way back to the rookery, but she can't hear him. She's still too far away. If the mother doesn't come back soon with food, the chick will die.

Two days pass before the mother can hear the father penguin's call.

At last the mother arrives at the rookery. She cuddles close to the chick and trumpets to him. He whistles back. With her beak she brushes his soft gray down.

The mother swallowed many fish before she left the ocean. She brings some of this food back up from her stomach and feeds her chick. She has enough food to keep him fed for weeks. He stays on her feet and snuggles into her brood patch.

The father is very hungry, so he travels to open water. There he dives to hunt for food. Weeks later the father returns with more food for the chick.

Each day the parents preen, or brush, the chick's downy coat with their beaks. This keeps the down fluffy and keeps the chick warm.

As the chick gets bigger, he and the other chicks no longer need to stay on their parents' feet. Instead they stay together to keep warm.

This group of chicks is called a *crèche,* or a nursery. The chick now spends most of his time here. But he still rushes to his mother or father to be fed when either one comes back from the ocean.

WINTER		**SPRING**
August	*September*	*October*

Sometimes the chick and the other young penguins dig their beaks into the ice to help them walk up a slippery hill. They toboggan down fast on their fluffy bellies.

The chick grows and grows. After five months, he has grown into a junior penguin. He is old enough to travel to the ocean.

November

December

SUMMER

January

Now he has a waterproof coat of feathers, instead of fluffy down. He can swim in the icy cold ocean because his feathers keep him dry and warm.

The young penguin spends most of his time in the water. He swims, flapping his flippers as if he were flying underwater. He uses his webbed feet to steer wherever he wants to go.

He catches a fish with his beak and swallows it headfirst.

Now the young penguin can catch his own food and take care of himself. In about five years he'll find a mate. Then he'll take care of his own egg until the chick can hatch.

Think, Talk and Write

Talk About It The author is like a reporter, telling you about the emperor penguins as if you and she were in Antarctica. Read page 182 aloud as if you are a reporter. How does the author make you feel as if you're there?

1. Use the pictures below to summarize what you learned. **Summarize**

2. Look back at page 189. What details support the idea that the penguin father and mother take care of the chick? **Main Idea and Details**

3. Did you use any reference sources to help you understand what you were reading? Which ones? If not, what sources could you have used? **Monitor and Clarify**

4. This story is about penguin chicks. If you wrote a paragraph about barnyard chicks, which words from the Words to Know list on p. 176 could you use? Try it. **Vocabulary**

Look Back and Write Look back at the question on page 181. Find information in the text about how penguins protect their chicks. Write a response to the question.

Meet author **Betty Tatham on page 451.**

Summarize

R2.5 Distinguish the main idea and supporting details in expository text.

Writing

Prompt *Penguin Chick* tells how the structure of a penguin's body helps it care for its young. Think about how the structure of an animal helps it solve problems. Now write an article for a pet magazine about the animal.

Writing Trait

Proper **conventions** are important when writing for an audience.

Student Model

Suited for the Desert

Unless you live in the desert you probably will never have a camel for a pet. If you did have one, however, you would find you don't have to do much to care for it.

An Arabian camel is suited in every way for living in the desert. If food is hard to find, it can live on energy from the fat in its hump. If water is scarce, it can survive for months without it.

In the Sahara Desert, a camel's eyes are protected from the hot sun by thick eyebrows. Long eyelashes keep out sand when the wind blows. Its ears are set far back on its head. The ears are covered with hair, even on the inside. This keeps out sand and dust.

Camels work hard and are often called "ships of the desert." But you probably shouldn't ask them to play with you. They are known to have very bad tempers.

Capitalize proper nouns and the first word in every sentence.

An article tells about real places and things.

Writer uses conventions correctly to make ideas clear.

Use the model to help you write your own magazine article.

Smart Solutions

G4W1.1 Select a focus, an organizational structure, and a point of view based on purpose, audience, length, and format requirements.

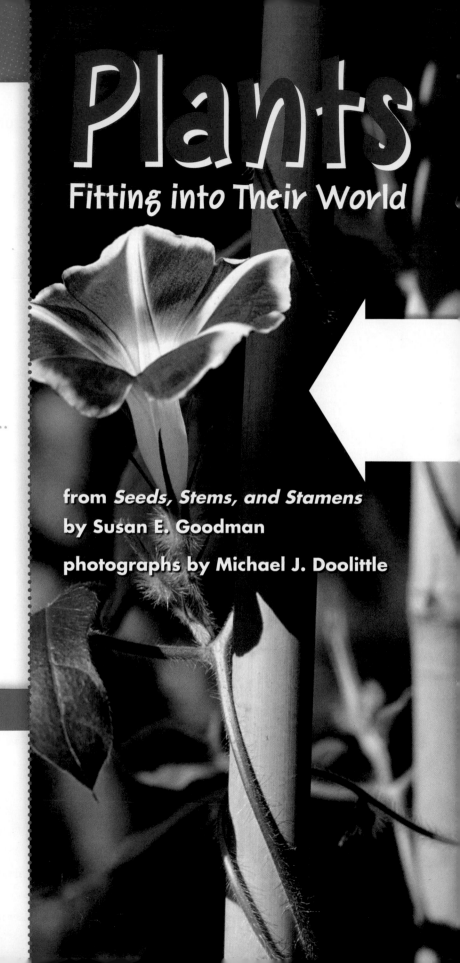

Skill Talk

Graphic Sources
are features that show
information visually,
or in a way you can
see. This photo essay
uses photographs of the
plants described in the text.
Arrows clearly show which
photo goes with each piece
of text. The name of each
plant is in bold type.

 Ready to Try It?
Before you read *Plants:
Fitting into Their World,*
look at the photographs
and think about what
information might be given
in the text. As you read the
photo essay, look at the
photos again to help you
understand the text.

Science Link

Use the library or the
Internet to find more
examples of ways that
plants get sunlight and
water. Report what you
find to the class.

Plants
Fitting into Their World

from *Seeds, Stems, and Stamens*
by **Susan E. Goodman**

photographs by **Michael J. Doolittle**

Getting Sun

Almost all plants need sun to live. They use a process called *photosynthesis* to turn sunlight into food or energy. But sometimes getting enough light can be a problem. Tall plants and trees get it by growing higher than those around them. To do so, they use a lot of energy growing a strong stem or trunk. Other plants have different ways to grab their share of sunshine.

Hitching a Ride

This **morning glory** spends its energy climbing instead. This vine uses its flexible stem to wind around strong objects and get to the light.

This **bromeliad** is a different kind of hitchhiker. It is an air plant. It grows high on a tree and uses its roots to anchor itself to the tree's trunk or upper branches.

Leaf Placement

Many plants arrange their leaves so they can get as much sun as possible. **Mint** leaves grow in crossed pairs. That way, the leaves cast less shadow upon their neighbors.

Getting Nutrients

Most plants get their nutrients from the soil. Some plants have evolved a different way to get their "vitamins."

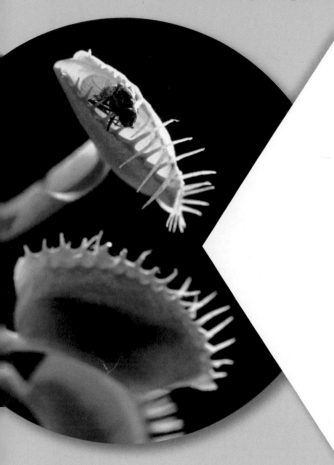

Meat-Eaters

The leaf tips of a **Venus's-flytrap** look very tempting to an insect. They are an easy place to land. They shine with what looks to be food. Mistake! Less than a second after a bug crawls in, the trap springs shut. The bristles on the leaves point outward to keep the insect from escaping as the trap closes. The plant then uses chemicals to digest its meal. In this picture, one leaf tip has just captured a fly, while a bigger leaf tip below is in the middle of digesting another.

The inventor of sticky flypaper might have gotten the idea from a **sundew plant.** A sundew's leaves are covered with hairs. And these hairs are covered with "sundew glue." The insect that lands on a sundew is there for good. It sticks to the hairs, which fold over and trap it.

Staying Safe

Plants can't run away from hungry insects and animals. They have developed other ways to protect themselves.

Physical Defenses

Freeloaders like bromeliads and vines don't directly harm their host tree, but they can do damage. They soak up water and sun that the tree could have used. If too many of them pile onto a tree, they can break off its branches. This **terminalia tree** has a great defense. Every so often, it sheds its bark—and with it, most of its unwanted company.

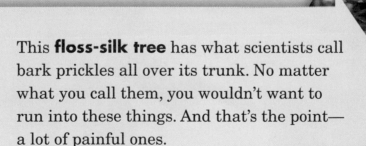

This **floss-silk tree** has what scientists call bark prickles all over its trunk. No matter what you call them, you wouldn't want to run into these things. And that's the point— a lot of painful ones.

Reading Across Texts
Which growing thing do you think has a harder time surviving—penguin chicks or the plants in this selection?

Writing Across Texts Create a chart to explain why you think as you do.

Let's Talk About
Good Solutions

LS1.7 Use clear and specific vocabulary to communicate ideas and establish the tone.

Build Vocabulary

Learn   ⊙ **Skill Unfamiliar Words** What do you do when you come across a word you don't know? First, read the words and sentences around the unfamiliar word. Sometimes the author explains what the word means. Look for context clues such as an example, a synonym, or a restatement.

Practice   Read "Wrong Turn" on page 203. As you read, use context clues to help you understand the meanings of the highlighted words.

Words to Know	lane	warned	smirked
	boomed	lurched	bounced
	crates		

On Your Own   Reread "Wrong Turn." Make a list of the highlighted words and the context clues that helped you know what each word means.

R1.6 Use sentence and word context to find the meaning of unknown words.

Wrong Turn

It was harvest time at my family's California vineyards. I was helping my older brother, Seth, deliver a truckload of grapes to a nearby town. Seth drove the old blue pickup truck down the quiet country roads.

At the junction, Seth turned the wheel and we headed left, down a narrow lane.

"Hey," I said. "Dad warned us not to go this way. He said this road is too rough."

Seth smirked and said, "Dad's not always right."

Suddenly the truck boomed and lurched to the left. The front wheel had bounced over a large hole. I looked into the back of the truck and saw that two crates of grapes had spilled.

"Seth," I said, "it looks like we might end up delivering grape jam instead of grapes." I pointed to the back of the truck.

The smug look disappeared from Seth's face when he saw the two empty wooden boxes. He stopped the truck and we cleaned up the mess. Then Seth drove the truck slowly and carefully into town.

When we got home, Seth told my dad what happened. My dad's voice was gentle when he spoke, "I hope you learned your lesson, Seth." I knew that was the last time Seth would take that route into town.

First Day in Grapes

 Need a Review?
See *Words!*, p. W•7 for more information about using context clues to find the meanings of unfamiliar words.

 Ready to Try It?
Read *First Day in Grapes*, pp. 206–219.

Smart Solutions

Build Comprehension

Learn ⊙ **Skill Main Idea and Details**

- A nonfiction paragraph is a group of sentences about the same subject or topic.

- The main idea of a paragraph is the most important idea about the topic. Sometimes the author tells the main idea, and sometimes the reader must figure out the main idea.

- Supporting details are small pieces of information that tell more about the main idea.

- Fiction stories are different from nonfiction. The main idea of a fiction story is what the story is all about in just a few words.

Practice Read "César Chávez" on page 205. This is a nonfiction passage. Look for the main idea in each paragraph.

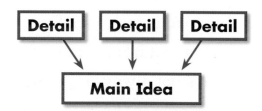

On Your Own **Write to Read** Reread "César Chávez." Use the graphic organizer above to show the main idea and supporting details from the second paragraph. In your own words, write a brief summary of Chávez's childhood.

- - - - - - - - - - - - - - - - - - - -

 Need a Review?
See *Picture It!*, p. PI•9 for more information about main idea and details.

 Ready to Try It?
As you read *First Day in Grapes*, pp. 206–219, look for details that help you understand what the story is all about.

R2.5 Distinguish the main idea and supporting details in expository text.

César Chávez

When César Chávez was a child in the 1930s and 1940s, his family moved thirty times. Like many other <u>migrant workers,</u> Chávez's parents earned a living by working in the fields of California. <u>Chávez's family moved from place to place,</u> looking for work. They picked lettuce in winter, beans in the spring, grapes in the summer, and cotton in the fall.

Life was very hard for migrant workers. They earned very little money. Sometimes the workers and their families did not have fresh water to drink or clean places to sleep.

When César Chávez grew up, he decided it was time for things to change. In 1962, he started a group called the National Farm Workers Association. Chávez and his group spoke about the bad conditions for workers in the fields. People listened and changes were made. Farm owners started paying the workers more money. The workers and their families had nicer places to live.

Skill The topic of this passage is César Chávez. You can combine the two underlined ideas into one sentence that tells the main idea: Chávez moved a lot when he was a child because his parents were migrant workers.

Skill Here is the main idea of the third paragraph. Can you find details that support it?

Smart Solutions

Realistic Fiction is a story that could really happen. Were you nervous about your first day of school?

First Day in Grapes

by L. King Pérez
illustrated by Robert Casilla

How does Chico feel
about his first day?

Chico never could decide if California reminded him of a fruit basket or a pizza. His family traveled from one migrant camp to another, picking fruits and vegetables.

They had arrived at a camp in grapes last night.

"Get up, Chico. Pronto," Mamá called as her hands patted the tortillas she was making for the family's meals. "You can't be late your first day. *Ándale.*" Let's go.

He'd had so many first days—first days in artichokes, first days in onions, first days in garlic. Now his first day in third grade would be in grapes.

"I don't want to go to school," Chico complained to Mamá when he went into the kitchen to wash. "Kids pick on me. They call me names."

"Listen," Mamá said. "We all have jobs, and school is yours."

Mamá put one hand on Chico's shoulder, the other on his back. She straightened him up until he looked like Papá before he went to work in the fields each day. Chico wondered why Mamá kept doing that. Sure as grapes turn purple, she stood him tall when he went to school.

When the bus came, the driver looked mean as a
crew boss.

"Hurry up!" the bus driver boomed before Chico or
the others could find places to sit. "Move it!"

The bus lurched forward. Chico grabbed the back of
a seat and held on.

"You better watch out or Old Hoonch will get you,"
the boy sitting there warned Chico.

Two boys in the first row bounced on their seats and
shoved each other.

"You better watch out for those troublemakers too,"
Chico's seatmate said. "Mike and Tony—they're mean
kids in fourth grade."

At school the office secretary told Chico to go to room 8. There, George Washington's picture hung above the chalkboard. Chico silently greeted his old friend from other schools. *Buenos días, amigo.*

The teacher's name was Ms. Andrews. "Welcome, Chico," she said. "You can sit there, by John Evans."

John looked friendlier than many of the kids he'd met in other schools.

Ms. Andrews asked the two new students to tell the class about themselves.

Sylvie, a girl from camp, stood and took a little bow.

"My name is Sylvie Castro," she said. "I have two brothers and two sisters, but I'd rather have a kitten." Everyone laughed, even Ms. Andrews.

Now Chico saw the whole class looking his way. George Washington too. Chico had to say something.

"I'm Chico Padilla. My papá picks more crates than his friends Juan Grande and Juan Chiquito together. He's real quick."

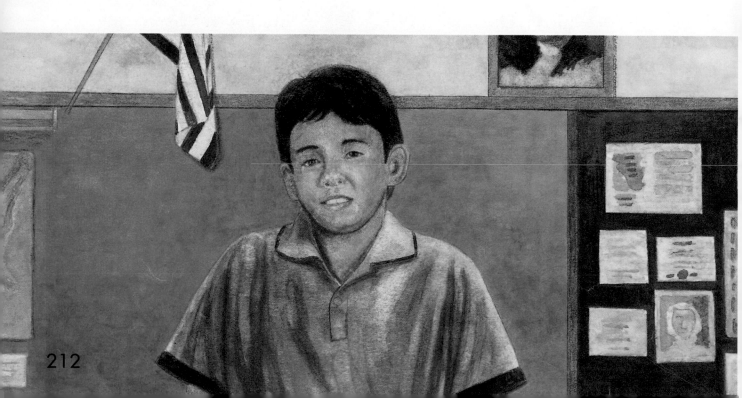

During math, Ms. Andrews called on Chico.

"Fourteen plus forty-five is…?" Ms. Andrews asked.

Chico picked up the chalk and wrote *59*. It was easy as adding the crates of fruits and vegetables Papá picked.

Ms. Andrews winked. "Let's try fifty-eight plus thirty-six."

In a flash Chico wrote *94*.

Ms. Andrews' eyebrows shot up. "Can you do fifty-nine plus ninety-four?"

Chico thought for a second. Then he wrote *153*.

"Oh, YES!" said Ms. Andrews, giving a thumbs-up.

Chico hadn't felt this good since he'd broken the piñata at the harvest picnic.

"I bet you'd like the Math Fair," John told Chico
when he got back to his desk. "It's next month."

This first day isn't so bad, Chico thought, sitting at a
lunch table.

Just then Mike and Tony, the troublemakers from
the bus, came over to Chico's table.

"Oh, yum, yum. Let's see what this new kid eats,"
Mike said, grabbing Chico's lunch sack.

"Looky here," said Tony, holding up a tortilla. "This
looks like cardboard. Bet it tastes like it too."

"Betcha his mommy makes them," Mike teased.

"Don't talk about my mamá," Chico warned in a low
voice.

"What'd you say?" Mike said.

That's when Chico felt Mamá's hands. Finally he got it!

Mamá meant for him to have courage, be strong. Although his knees felt weak, Chico stood up tall.

It got quiet enough to hear cucumbers grow.

Tony leaned so close, Chico could feel his breath. Then Tony pointed his finger and smirked. "Well, look who's trying to be macho."

Chico didn't feel macho, and he didn't feel brave either. He wished he were back at the chalkboard, working math problems.

Suddenly Chico said, "Do *you* know what fifty-nine and ninety-four is?"

"WHAT?!" Mike and Tony said together. They looked surprised.

"One hundred fifty-three," Chico replied.

"Need an easier one? What if you take sixty-five crates of dried grapes and add seventy-seven crates to it? How many crates of raisins do you get?" Chico continued.

A crowd of kids began to surround them.

"Leave him alone," a girl called out.

"He didn't do anything to you," someone else added.

Tony looked around. "This is dumb," he said. "Who cares about adding up crates."

"Yeah. Who cares," repeated Mike.

No one moved. No one said a word. Finally Mike and Tony turned, trying to look tough. The crowd parted, letting them walk through.

John rushed over to Chico. "Those kids scare everybody," said John. "But you didn't look scared."

"They scared me some," Chico admitted, but he thought, *Bravo!* He stood up for himself, and it felt good.

That afternoon, getting off the bus, Chico walked past Old Hoonch.

"Buenas tardes y gracias," Chico said.

Old Hoonch glared at him. "What'd you say?"

"I said, 'Good afternoon and thank you.' You know, for the ride." He took a deep breath. "And my name is Chico. Chico Padilla. I live here now, in grapes."

Old Hoonch rested his elbow on the steering wheel and looked down Chico's lane. "Well, good afternoon to you, Chico Padilla," he mumbled. "See you tomorrow."

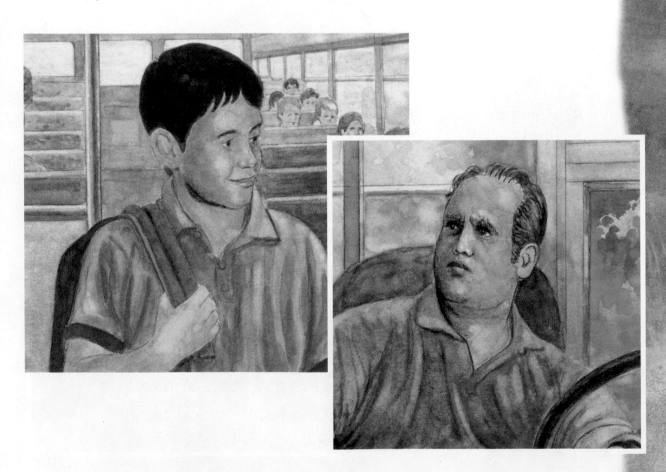

Chico jumped off the bus. This had been a pretty good first day. He had a new friend and a good teacher, and Old Hoonch knew his name.

Think, Talk and Write

Talk About It At the end of his first day of third grade, Chico feels he had "a pretty good first day." What do you think will happen the next day? How do you think Chico will feel after a week at his new school?

1. Use the pictures below to retell the story. **Retell**

2. What is *First Day in Grapes* all about? Find details in the story that support your answer. **Main Idea and Details**

3. What did you predict would happen when Mike and Tony began teasing Chico at lunch? What clues in the story helped you make your prediction? **Predict**

4. Pretend you are Chico. Write a journal entry about your first day at school. Use words from the Words to Know list on p. 202. **Vocabulary**

Look Back and Write Look back at the question on page 207. Think about how Chico feels at different times in the story. Then choose one picture of Chico from the story. Write a paragraph telling how Chico felt in that picture. Be sure to include details from the story to support your answer.

Meet author L. King Pérez on page 450 and illustrator Robert Casilla on page 447.

Retell

R3.2 Comprehend basic plots of classic fairy tales, myths, folktales, legends, and fables from around the world.

Writing · Realistic Story

Prompt *First Day in Grapes* is a realistic story about a boy who solves a problem at school. Think about another problem Chico may have at school. Now write a realistic story about how Chico solves this problem.

Writing Trait

Organize your story in paragraphs.

Student Model

The Science Test

There was only one week left until Chico and John's big Science test. John was really good at Science, but no matter how much Chico studied, he always struggled with the tests.

John offered to help Chico study. Everyday after school, John came over and studied with Chico. John created sample tests for Chico to practice with. They made flash cards used them to quiz each other.

Finally, it was the day of the big test. Chico wasn't as nervous as he thought he'd be. John's help made Chico feel prepared for the test. Chico flipped his paper over and looked at all of the questions. He knew the answers! He finished his test and turned it in. He couldn't wait to get the test back.

A few days later, Mr. Jones, the Science teacher, passed the tests back. Chico couldn't believe his eyes. He got an A! His hard work paid off.

Plural nouns refer to more than one person, place, or thing.

A realistic story tells about something that could happen in real life.

The writer organizes events in time order to make the story easy to follow.

Use the model to help you write your own realistic story.

G2W1.1 Group related ideas and maintain a consistent focus.
W2.1.b Write narratives: Include well-chosen details to develop the plot.

Smart Solutions

221

E-Mail The letter *e* in *e-mail* stands for *electronic*. An e-mail is a message sent by computer over the Internet from one user to another. E-mail lets you communicate with people all over the world. The *To:* box shows to whom a message is going. The message itself looks like the body of a letter.

 Ready to Try It?
As you read "The Big Soccer Game," read the captions to help you understand how an e-mail is organized.

Social Studies Link

Think about a special talent or skill you have. How do you use your special ability in school? Write an advertisement that tells your classmates about your special skill or talent you have.

The Big Soccer Game

Francisco and Jose used to attend school together until Jose moved. They also played together on the soccer team. Jose knows Francisco needs some encouragement and support because he has a big soccer game coming up. Even though the two friends do not go to the same school anymore, they can keep in touch using e-mail.

for more practice
Get Online!
PearsonSuccessNet.com

Francisco used his e-mail provider to write to his friend Jose.

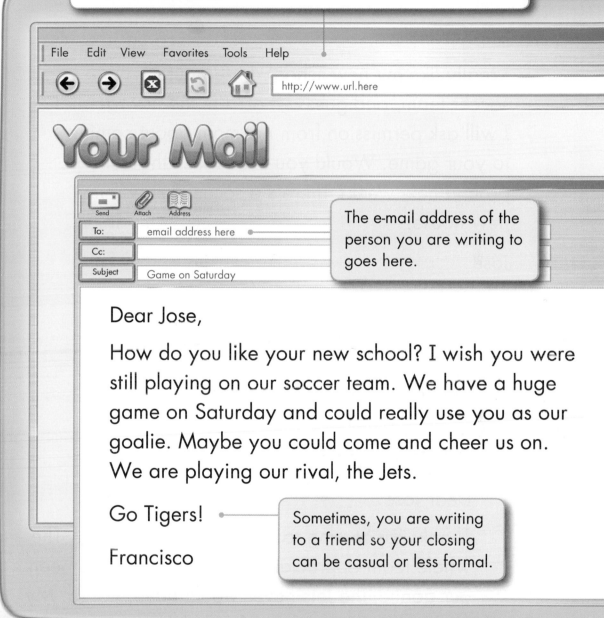

File   Edit   View   Favorites   Tools   Help

http://www.url.here

Your Mail

Send   Attach   Address

To: email address here

Cc:

Subject   Game on Saturday

The e-mail address of the person you are writing to goes here.

Dear Jose,

How do you like your new school? I wish you were still playing on our soccer team. We have a huge game on Saturday and could really use you as our goalie. Maybe you could come and cheer us on. We are playing our rival, the Jets.

Go Tigers!

Francisco

Sometimes, you are writing to a friend so your closing can be casual or less formal.

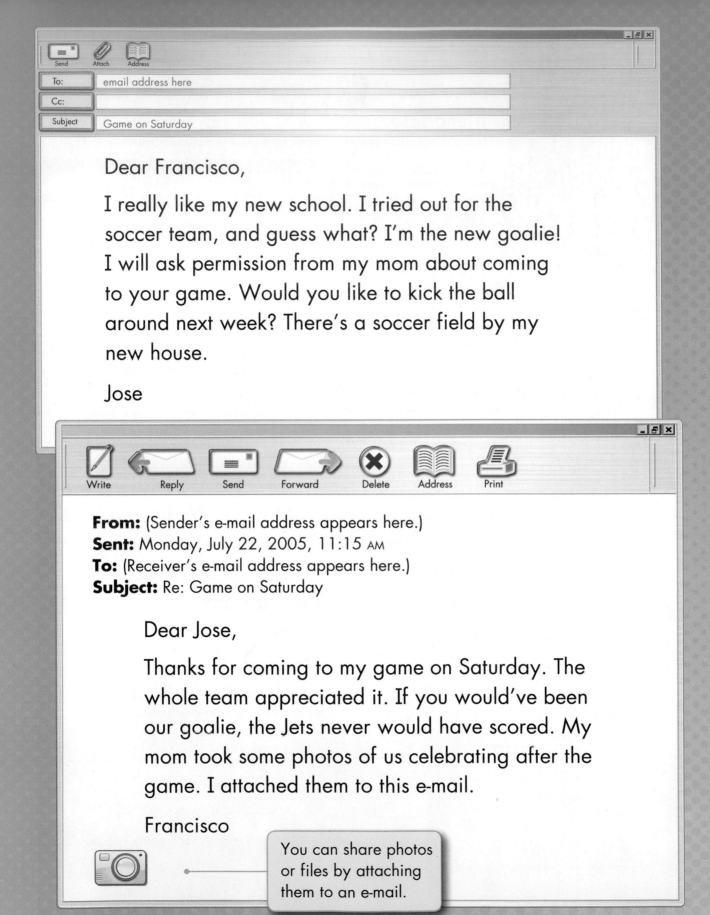

Subject: Game on Saturday

Dear Francisco,

I really like my new school. I tried out for the soccer team, and guess what? I'm the new goalie! I will ask permission from my mom about coming to your game. Would you like to kick the ball around next week? There's a soccer field by my new house.

Jose

From: (Sender's e-mail address appears here.)
Sent: Monday, July 22, 2005, 11:15 AM
To: (Receiver's e-mail address appears here.)
Subject: Re: Game on Saturday

Dear Jose,

Thanks for coming to my game on Saturday. The whole team appreciated it. If you would've been our goalie, the Jets never would have scored. My mom took some photos of us celebrating after the game. I attached them to this e-mail.

Francisco

You can share photos or files by attaching them to an e-mail.

Jose was really excited. He clicked on the icon and found these photos.

Reading Across Texts

Do you think Jose would like to be friends with Chico from *First Day in Grapes*? What do the two boys have in common?

Writing Across Texts Pretend that you are Jose and you just moved to Chico's school. Write an e-mail to Chico introducing yourself.

Let's Talk About
Finding Solutions

LS1.7 Use clear and specific vocabulary to communicate ideas and establish the tone.

Build Vocabulary

Learn ⊙ **Skill Compound Words** are two small words put together to make a new word. You can use the meanings of the two smaller words to find the meaning of a compound word. For example, *lunchroom* is the room where you have lunch.

Practice Read "Get Organized" on page 229. As you read, search for compound words. Think about the meaning of each small word in the compound words.

Words to Know	enormous	scattered	strain
	collection	butterflies	shoelaces

On Your Own Reread "Get Organized." Write the compound words you find in the passage. Now list four other compound words that name things you might find around the house.

G2R1.8 Use knowledge of individual words in unknown compound words to predict their meaning.

Get Organized

Are there **enormous** piles of stuff in your room? Are your things **scattered** everywhere? Is your closet clutter putting a **strain** on the door? Then it's time to take action!

First, understand that this will take time and work. Look at each thing. Ask yourself, "Do I use this? Will I ever use this?" This information will help you decide what to get rid of and what to keep. Then look at the things you've decided not to keep. Are they in good shape? Give them away to a charity.

If not, put them in trash bags and throw them out.

Next, take the things you are keeping. Put them into groups. Put each group together in one place. Put all the books on a shelf or table. Hang the clothes in the closet or put them in drawers. Do you have a **collection** of objects, such as rocks, **butterflies**, or **shoelaces**? Display them together on a shelf, table, or wall.

Now vacuum and dust your room. Congratulations! You now have a clean, well-organized room.

 Need a Review?
See *Words!*, p. W•9 for more information about compound words.

 Ready to Try It?
Read *Prudy's Problem*, pp. 232–247.

Prudy's Problem and How She Solved It

Build Comprehension

Learn ⊙ **Skill Main Idea and Details**

- The main idea of a fictional story answers the question, "What is this story all about?"

- A nonfiction paragraph is a group of sentences that give information about the same subject or topic.

- Supporting details are small pieces of information that tell about the main idea.

Practice Read "Collecting Stamps" on page 231. It is a nonfiction passage. Look for the main idea of each paragraph.

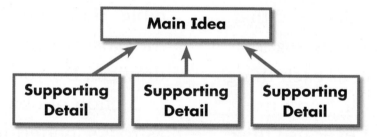

```
                    ┌─────────────────┐
                    │    Main Idea    │
                    └─────────────────┘
            ↗              ↑              ↖
┌──────────────┐  ┌──────────────┐  ┌──────────────┐
│  Supporting  │  │  Supporting  │  │  Supporting  │
│    Detail    │  │    Detail    │  │    Detail    │
└──────────────┘  └──────────────┘  └──────────────┘
```

On Your Own **Write to Read** Reread "Collecting Stamps." Use the graphic organizer above to show the main idea and supporting details of both the third and fourth paragraphs. Then write a short paragraph in your own words explaining two solutions to the problem discussed the second paragraph.

 Need a Review? See *Picture It!*, p. PI•9 for more information about main idea and details.

 Ready to Try It? Read *Prudy's Problem,* pp. 232–247. As you read, look for details that help you understand the story.

🐻 R2.5 Distinguish the main idea and supporting details in expository text.

Collecting Stamps

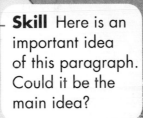

Collecting stamps is a fun and interesting hobby. Sometimes children and young people are interested in collecting stamps. But they might not have a lot of money to buy stamps. How can you get stamps without spending money?

There are a few ways you can solve that problem. One way is to ask people to give you stamps that they don't need. Start by telling all your friends and all the people in your family that you are starting to collect stamps. Suppose your uncle gets a letter from France. He can save the stamp and give it to you!

Another way to get stamps is to trade them with other people. Once you start collecting, you'll find that you will get more than one copy of the same stamp. Then you can use the copies to trade with other people for stamps that you don't have.

Asking people to save stamps for you and trading stamps are two good ways to get stamps. Before you know it, you'll have more stamps than you can count!

Skill Here is an important idea of this paragraph. Could it be the main idea?

Skill This sentence tells the main idea of the entire passage.

Prudy's Problem

and How She Solved It

by Carey Armstrong-Ellis

What happens when Prudy's problem gets out of control?

Prudy seemed like a normal little girl. She had a sister. She had a dog. She had two white mice. She had a mom and a dad and her own room at home.

Yes, Prudy seemed normal.

But Prudy collected things.

Now most kids collect something. Prudy's friend Egbert collected butterflies. So did Prudy.

Belinda had a stamp collection. So did Prudy.

Harold collected tin foil and made it into a big ball. So did Prudy.

All her friends had collections. And so did Prudy— but Prudy collected *everything*.

She saved rocks, feathers, leaves, twigs, dead bugs, and old flowers. She kept a box full of interesting fungi in the bottom drawer of her dresser. She saved every picture she had ever drawn and every valentine she had ever gotten. She saved pretty paper napkins from parties and kept them in her desk drawer. She had six hundred and fourteen stuffed animals in different unnatural colors.

She had collections of ribbons, shoelaces, souvenir postcards, flowered fabric scraps, pencils with fancy ends, pink scarves with orange polka dots, old calendars, salt and pepper shakers with faces, dried-out erasers, plastic lizards, pointy sunglasses, china animals, heart-shaped candy boxes with the paper candy cups still inside, tufts of hair from different breeds of dogs. . . .

She just could not throw anything away.

It drove her dad to distraction. He was a very tidy person who did not like clutter. He started saying unpleasant things as he tried to mow the lawn.

"Prudy, you have a problem," he said.

"What do you mean?" she asked, baffled.

"You just have too much stuff. Why don't we haul it all to the dump?" he suggested hopefully.

"I don't have too much stuff, Dad," Prudy said.

It even got to be too much for her mom, who did not mind clutter but could no longer navigate the living room.

"Maybe you could take all this to the thrift shop," she said. "Surely someone could use this old mushroom. . . ."

"I *like* that mushroom," Prudy said.

"Prudy, you have to face your problem," said her mother.

"I do not have a problem," said Prudy.

Prudy's little sister started putting together collections of her own.

"Uh–oh," said Egbert, eyeing Evie's little piles of pine twigs and used toothbrushes. "Prudy, how about if you packed everything all up and stuffed it into a rocket and sent it to Neptune?"

"Yeah, that would solve your problem!" agreed Harold and Belinda.

"There is no problem!" shouted Prudy.

But Prudy herself found that she could barely get to her desk to feed her mice.

She could not even get out of her room without setting off an avalanche of one thing or another.

And then one day while Prudy was walking home from school, something shiny caught her eye. It was a silver gum wrapper.

"I must take this home for my shiny things collection!" she thought.

She ran home and tried to squeeze it into her room.

Something started to happen. The walls started to bulge.

The door started to strain at the hinges.

The pressure was building higher . . . and higher. . . .

The room exploded with an enormous

BANG!

Bits and pieces of stuff flew everywhere.

"Holy smokes," said Prudy. "I guess maybe I do have a little problem."

For six weeks, everyone pitched in to gather Prudy's scattered collections.

"Now what, Prudy?" said her family.

"Now what, Prudy?" said her friends.

"I'm working on it!" said Prudy.

Prudy looked around for inspiration. She visited an art collection. She visited a fish collection. She visited a rock collection. She went to the library to find ideas.

At last, after many hours of scrutinizing stacks of books, she came up with a brilliant plan!

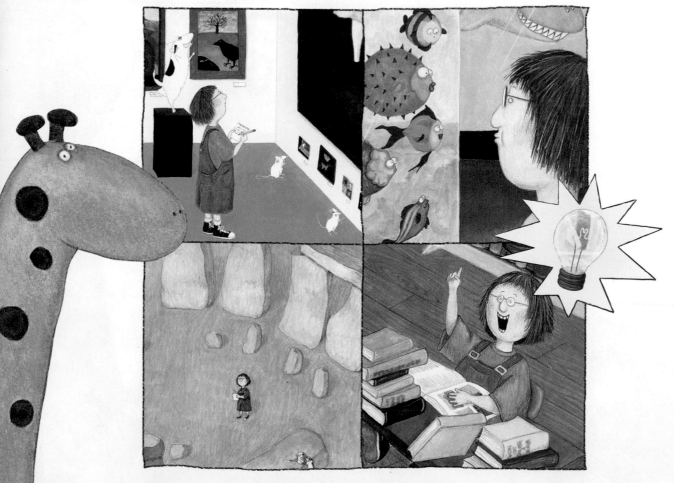

With saws whirring and hammers pounding, everyone set to work.

The Prudy Museum of Indescribable Wonderment
was an amazing sight to behold.

Everyone wanted to go visit!

Within a year, it was the biggest tourist attraction in
Prudy's town.

"Look at that, Egbert," said Belinda. "Did you ever
realize how many kinds of gym socks there are?"

"I had no idea cheese rinds could be so fascinating!"
said Prudy's mother.

"Can I go to the gift shop?" said Evie.

At last Prudy's collections were neat and orderly and appreciated by everyone. Now she could sit back and enjoy the museum and all her happy visitors. . . .

But she could never *really* stop collecting!

Think, Talk and Write

Talk About It The museum is getting full. Soon Prudy may need a new solution to her problem. Think of two solutions from which Prudy can choose.

1. Use the pictures below to retell the story. **Retell**

2. At the end of the story, Prudy learned something important. What did she learn? **Main Idea and Details**

3. Do you have a collection at home? Did you use what you know about collecting things to help you understand Prudy's story? **Prior Knowledge**

4. *Prudy's huge group of things flew all over.* Rewrite this sentence using words from the Words to Know list on p. 228. **Vocabulary**

TEST PRACTICE ★

Look Back and Write Look back at the question on page 233. Think about what made Prudy realize she had a problem. Also think about her creative solution. Now write a response to the question. Be sure to include details from the selection to support your answer.

Meet author and illustrator Carey Armstrong-Ellis on page 447.

Retell

R3.2 Comprehend basic plots of classic fairy tales, myths, folktales, legends, and fables from around the world.

Writing Fantasy

Prompt In *Prudy's Problem,* Prudy has to find a solution to a problem. Think about a problem that needs to be solved. Now write a fantasy in which you solve that problem.

Student Model

Me First!

One day I was sitting in the garden thinking. I felt annoyed with my little brother. Mark always wants to be first. Whether we're playing a game, going outside, or brushing our teeth, he always says, "Me first!" So I was trying to figure out what to do.

Suddenly I heard a tiny voice. "Hello," said the voice. I turned and saw a smiling butterfly perched on a flower petal! "I know how to solve your problem," she said.

Then she flew closer. She whispered in my ear, "Next time, tell Mark this little rhyme: Bekka tekka switcheroo. I'll be one and you be two." Before I could say thank you, she fluttered away.

I went inside and found Mark. I asked if he wanted to play Go Fish. "Me first!" Mark said.

Next I repeat the rhyme. "Bekka tekka switcheroo. I'll be one and you be two."

Mark looked surprised. "I mean, do you want to go first?" he asked. It worked! We played two games. I let Mark be first in the second game.

Some nouns have an irregular spelling.

A talking butterfly is an example of a make-believe story trait.

Only essential details are included in the story.

Use the model to help you write your own fantasy.

G4W1.3 Use traditional structures for conveying information (e.g., chronological order, cause and effect, similarity and difference, and posing and answering a question).

249

Smart Solutions

Classifying and categorizing means to put things that are related into groups. At the beginning of this interview, Dr. Feinman names some categories of objects in the Field Museum's anthropology collection. The photos show examples of objects in these categories.

 Ready to Try It?
Read "Meeting the Challenge of Collecting." As you read and look at the photos, think about how each of the objects shown in the photos could be classified or categorized.

Social Studies Link

Think about what you know about the history of your community and what you would like to learn. Make a KWL chart to organize your ideas. Now plan a visit to a museum or historical society in your area where you could learn more about your community's past.

MEETING THE CHALLENGE OF COLLECTING

BY LISA KLOBUCHAR

The Field Museum of Natural History, in Chicago, is one of the world's biggest museums. Dr. Gary Feinman is the head of the Field Museum's anthropology department. Anthropology is the study of how people live. Anthropologists look at how people fit in with the places they live. They study how different groups of people are alike and different. Dr. Feinman explains how the museum puts together its anthropology collections. He also talks about some of the challenges of putting these collections on display and how the museum meets these challenges.

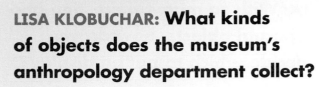

Dr. Gary Feinman

LISA KLOBUCHAR: What kinds of objects does the museum's anthropology department collect?

DR. FEINMAN: We have everything from tapestries to blow guns, from pottery to stone sculpture, from paintings to masks.

LK: That's quite a variety! How many objects does the museum own in all?

DR. F: Our department alone has over one million objects.

LK: Wow! How do you manage to display that many objects?

DR. F: Only a small part of the museum's anthropology collection is on display. We put out about one or two objects out of every one hundred. We don't have the space to display them all.

Incan pottery from Peru

251

LK: With so many interesting and unusual objects, how do you decide which to put on display?

DR. F: Our permanent displays all have certain themes. If an object fits in with that theme, we try to put it on display.

LK: Are there any objects that you would like to display but can't?

DR. F: Yes. Some objects are just too easily damaged. Some can be harmed by getting too hot or too cold. Others may be harmed by bright light or by air that is too moist or too dry. Moths or other insects can ruin cloth items and baskets.

Tapa bark cloth from Papua New Guinea

Woven basket of the Wappo Indians

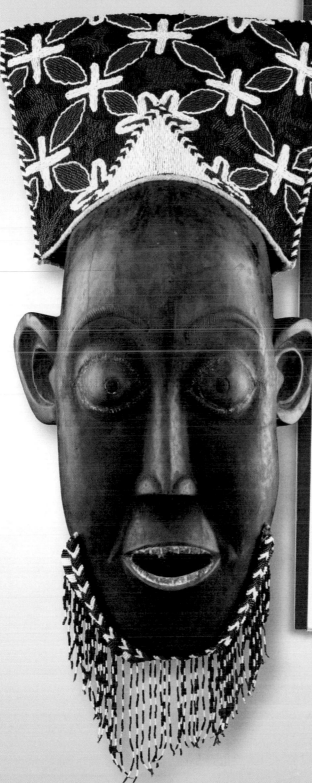

Mask from Cameroon

LK: Sounds like a real problem. How do you protect these objects?

DR. F: We have a full-time staff to care for our collection. They make sure the objects are stored properly. The Field Museum is building an underground collections center. This center will allow the museum to store objects safely. Caring for the collection is like caring for one's health. It is better to avoid problems than to look for a cure after big problems arise.

Reading Across Texts

How are Prudy's museum and the Field Museum of Natural History alike? How are they different?

Writing Across Texts Make a chart in which you show how the two museums are alike and different.

Let's Talk About
Fair Solutions

LS1.7 Use clear and specific vocabulary to communicate ideas and establish the tone.

Build Vocabulary

Learn ⊙ **Skill Antonyms** are words that have opposite meanings. For example, *empty* is the opposite of *full*. When you find an unfamiliar word in your reading, look for words that seem to mean the opposite. If you can find an antonym, it will help you figure out the meaning of the unfamiliar word.

Practice Read "Farming" on page 257. As you read, look for antonyms to help you understand the meanings of the highlighted words. If you need more help, use a dictionary or your glossary.

Words to Know	lazy	bottom	crops
	clever	cheated	partners
	wealth		

On Your Own Reread "Farming." Then write two sentences. In each sentence, use a word from the Words to Know list and its antonym.

256 🐻 **R1.4** Use knowledge of antonyms, synonyms, homophones, and homographs to determine the meanings of words. **R1.6** Use sentence and word context to find the meaning of unknown words.

Farming

Farming is not an occupation for lazy people. Farmers are always busy. In the spring they till, or turn up, the soil to prepare it for planting. Then they dig holes, put the seeds in the bottom of each hole, and cover them with soil. In the summer, farmers water and weed the growing crops. In the fall, it is time for harvesting. Then they cut or dig up the crops in the fields. In some countries, farmers use machines to do these things. In many countries, however, farmers still do many jobs by hand.

The weather can make any farmer look clever or foolish. Too much rain and the crops wash away; not enough rain and the crops die. The weather has often cheated farmers and ruined their crops. So farmers must be partners with the weather.

Most farmers do not make a lot of money. So why do they farm? Some farm to get the food they need. Many choose to be farmers because to them wealth is not as important as working with the land.

 Need a Review?
See *Words!*, p. W•2 for more information about antonyms.

 Ready to Try It?
Read *Tops and Bottoms*, pp. 260–277.

Build Comprehension

Learn ◉ **Skill Compare and Contrast**

- When you make a comparison, you tell how two or more things are alike and how they are different.

- When you make a contrast, you tell *only* how the things are different.

Practice Read "The Grasshopper and the Ant" on page 259.
Look for contrasts between the two characters.

	Grasshopper	**Ant**
What he does in summer		
What he does in winter		
A word that describes him		

On Your Own **Write to Read** Reread "The Grasshopper and the Ant." Make a chart like the one above. Fill in the chart with details from the passage. Now write a short paragraph contrasting Ant and Grasshopper.

 Need a Review?
See *Picture It!*, p. PI•5 for more practice with comparing and contrasting.

 Ready to Try It?
As you read *Tops and Bottoms*, pp. 260–277, look for ways in which the main characters are alike and different.

  R3.3 Determine what characters are like by what they say or do and by how the author or illustrator portrays them.

THE *Grasshopper* AND THE *Ant*

A retelling of an Aesop fable

On a warm summer day, Grasshopper sat in the shade and chirped. Ant walked up carrying some corn.

"Ant," said Grasshopper. "What are you doing working in the hot summer sun? Come relax in the shade with me."

Skill Here is a difference between the two characters. Grasshopper is relaxing while Ant is working.

"I can't," said Ant. "There is work to be done! I am storing food for the winter, and I suggest you do the same."

"Winter?" said Grasshopper. "That's a long time away. I can't be bothered about winter in the middle of summer! Are you sure you won't sit in this lovely shade with me?"

Ant just picked up the corn and went back to work.

Winter came, and the ground was cold and bare. Grasshopper had no food and lay under a bush. *I'm dying of hunger!* he thought. Nearby, the ants were eating the corn they had stored last summer. When they saw Grasshopper, they dragged some food over to him.

Skill This paragraph tells another difference between Grasshopper and Ant. You could write it in your chart.

Grasshopper learned an important lesson. Next summer would be different.

An **animal fantasy** is a story with animal characters that behave like people. Look for ways that Bear and Hare act like people.

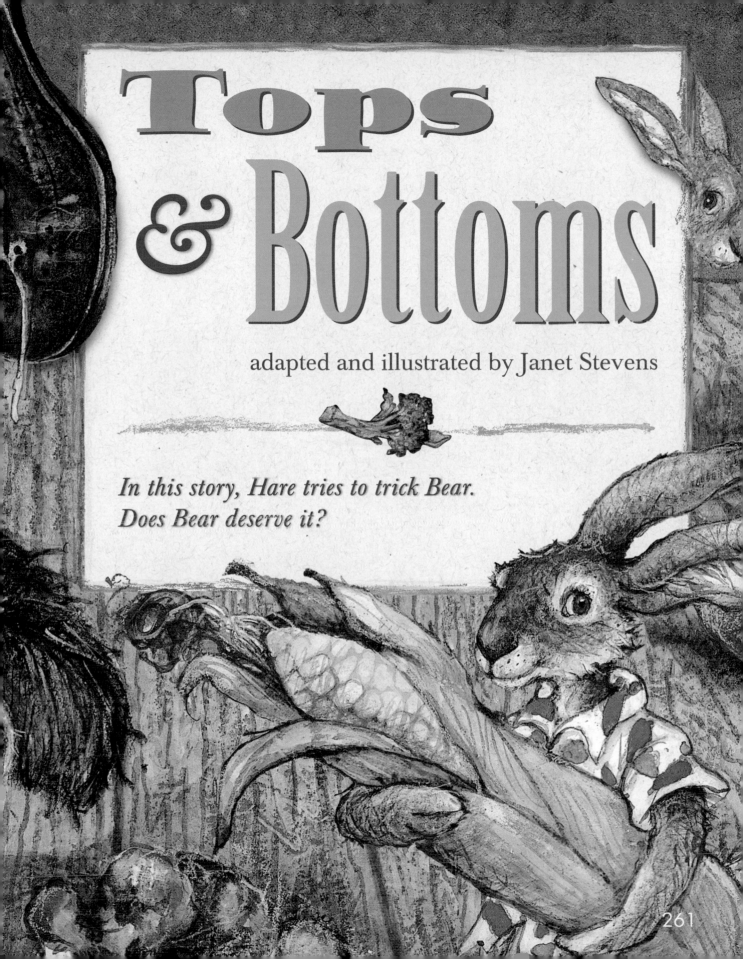

Tops & Bottoms

adapted and illustrated by Janet Stevens

*In this story, Hare tries to trick Bear.
Does Bear deserve it?*

Once upon a time there lived a very lazy bear who had lots of money and lots of land. His father had been a hard worker and a smart business bear, and he had given all of his wealth to his son.

But all Bear wanted to do was sleep.

Not far down the road lived a hare. Although Hare was clever, he sometimes got into trouble. He had once owned land, too, but now he had nothing. He had lost a risky bet with a tortoise and had sold all of his land to Bear to pay off the debt.

Hare and his family were in very bad shape.

"The children are so hungry, Father Hare! We must think of something!" Mrs. Hare cried one day. So Hare and Mrs. Hare put their heads together and cooked up a plan.

The next day Hare hopped down the road to Bear's house. Bear, of course, was asleep.

"Hello, Bear, wake up! It's your neighbor, Hare, and I have an idea!"

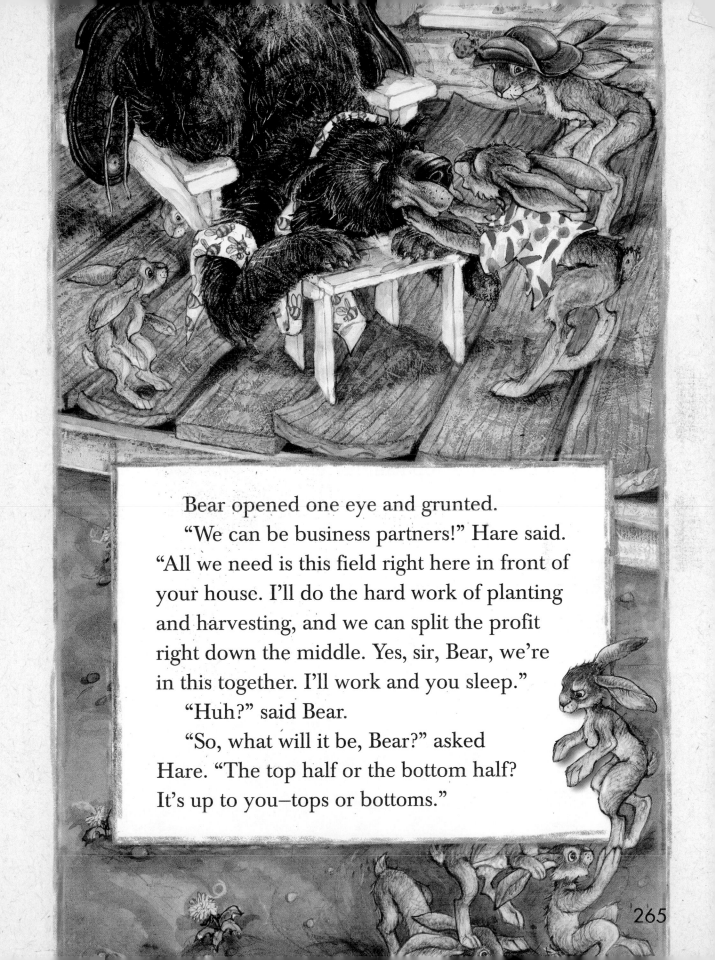

Bear opened one eye and grunted.

"We can be business partners!" Hare said. "All we need is this field right here in front of your house. I'll do the hard work of planting and harvesting, and we can split the profit right down the middle. Yes, sir, Bear, we're in this together. I'll work and you sleep."

"Huh?" said Bear.

"So, what will it be, Bear?" asked Hare. "The top half or the bottom half? It's up to you—tops or bottoms."

"Uh, let's see," Bear said with a yawn.
"I'll take the top half, Hare. Right–tops."
Hare smiled. "It's a done deal, Bear."
So Bear went back to sleep, and Hare
and his family went to work. Hare planted,
Mrs. Hare watered, and everyone weeded.

Bear slept as the crops grew.

When it was time for the harvest, Hare called out, "Wake up, Bear! You get the tops and I get the bottoms."

Hare and his family dug up the carrots,
the radishes, and the beets. Hare plucked off
all the tops, tossed them into a pile for Bear,
and put the bottoms aside for himself.

Bear stared at his pile. "But, Hare, all the best parts are in your half!"

"You chose the tops, Bear," Hare said.

"Now, Hare, you've tricked me. You plant this field again—and this season I want the bottoms!"

Hare agreed. "It's a done deal, Bear."

So Bear went back to sleep, and Hare and his family went to work. They planted, watered, and weeded.

Bear slept as the crops grew.

When it was time for the harvest, Hare called out, "Wake up, Bear! You get the bottoms and I get the tops."

Hare and his family gathered up the lettuce, the broccoli, and the celery. Hare pulled off the bottoms for Bear and put the tops in his own pile.

Bear looked at his pile and scowled. "Hare, you have cheated me again."

"But, Bear," Hare said, "you wanted the bottoms this time."

Bear growled, "You plant this field again, Hare. You've tricked me twice, and you owe me one season of both tops and bottoms!"

"You're right, poor old Bear," sighed Hare. "It's only fair that you get both tops and bottoms this time. It's a done deal, Bear."

So Bear went back to sleep, and Hare and his family went to work. They planted, watered, and weeded, then watered and weeded some more.

Bear slept as the crops grew.

When it was time for the harvest, Hare called out, "Wake up, Bear! This time you get the tops and the bottoms!"

There in front of Bear's house lay a high field of corn. Hare and his family yanked up every cornstalk. Hare tugged off the roots at the bottom and the tassels at the top and put them in a pile for Bear. Then he carefully collected the ears of corn in the middle and placed them in his own pile.

Bear rubbed his eyes and watched.

"See, Bear? You get the tops and the bottoms. I get the middles. Yes, sir, Bear. It's a done deal!"

By now Bear was wide awake. "That's it, Hare!" he hollered. "From now on I'll plant my own crops and take the tops, bottoms, and middles!"

Hare and his family scooped up the corn and hopped down the road toward home.

Bear never again slept through a season of planting and harvesting. Hare bought back his land with the profit from the crops, and he and Mrs. Hare opened a vegetable stand.

And although Hare and Bear learned to live happily as neighbors, they never became business partners again!

Think, Talk and Write

Talk About It Some people are like the characters in this story. Are you more like Bear or Hare? Tell why.

1. Use the pictures below to retell the story. **Retell**

2. Bear and Hare are very different from each other. Make a Venn diagram to compare and contrast them. Label the circles *Bear* and *Hare*. Label the middle section *Both*. Fill in the diagram. **Compare and Contrast**

3. What did you predict would happen after the first harvest? How did that prediction help you with your next prediction? **Predict**

4. Bear and Hare both had problems at the beginning of the story. What were their problems and how were they resolved at the end of the story? Use words from the Words to Know list on p. 256 to write your answer. **Vocabulary**

TEST PRACTICE **Look Back and Write** Look back at the question on page 261. Do you think Bear deserved to be tricked? Why or why not? Be sure to include details from the story to support your answer.

Meet author and illustrator Janet Stevens on page 450.

Retell

R3.3 Determine what characters are like by what they say or do and by how the author or illustrator portrays them.

Writing

Prompt *Tops and Bottoms* is a fantasy about animals trying to find a fair solution to their problem. Think about a problem that animals might face. Now write a fantasy in which these animals solve their problem.

> **Writing Trait**
>
> A strong, lively **voice** will entertain your readers.

Student Model

Hoppy and Floppy

Hoppy and Floppy are little rabbits. They love to eat berries. One day they went to their favorite place to pick raspberries. But some crows were already there, eating all the fruit! Floppy's grandmother grew blueberries, but her house was too far away for the rabbits to go. So Hoppy told the birds how to get to the blueberries. She asked them to bring some back for her and Floppy. The birds agreed and they flew off. Soon they returned with a basket full of blueberries. The birds and rabbits shared the sweet, delicious fruit.

A possessive noun includes an apostrophe and the letter *s*.

Animal characters can do impossible things, such as talk.

The writer includes interesting details to give the story a lively voice.

Use the model to help you write your own fantasy.

W2.1.b Write narratives: Include well-chosen details to develop the plot.

Smart Solutions

279

Text Structures are ways that authors organize information to help readers understand the text. Authors often use a compare-and-contrast text structure when explaining how two or more things are alike and different. In this fable, the first sentence tells a difference between the two main characters.

 Ready to Try It?
Read *The Hare and the Tortoise*. Look for comparisons and contrasts the author makes about the two main characters.

Social Studies Link

Think about the Hare and the Tortoise. If they were people, which one do you think would be a better student? Why? Write a short paragraph explaining your answer. Then share your paragraph with your class.

The Hare and the Tortoise

by Aesop
illustrated by Michael Hague

One day a quick-footed Hare was making fun of a slow-moving Tortoise. Much to the Hare's surprise, the Tortoise began to laugh. "I challenge you to a race," said the Tortoise, "and I bet that I will win."

"Very well," said the Hare, "I will dance rings around you all the way."

It was soon agreed that the Fox would set the course and be the judge. The race began and the Hare ran so quickly that he soon left the Tortoise far behind. Once he reached the middle of the course, the Hare decided to take a nap.

While the Hare slept, the Tortoise plodded on and on, straight toward the finish line. When the Hare awoke from his nap, he was surprised that the Tortoise was nowhere in sight. Racing to the finish line as fast as he could, the Hare was shocked to find the Tortoise waiting for him with a smile on his face.

Slow and steady wins the race.

Reading Across Texts
Who were the winner and the loser in this story and in *Tops and Bottoms*? Why did the winner win each time?

Writing Across Texts Write a short paragraph comparing the winners.

Let's Talk About
Plant and Animal Adaptations

LS1.7 Use clear and specific vocabulary to communicate ideas and establish the tone.

Build Vocabulary

Learn   ⊙ **Skill Unfamiliar Words** If you find a word you do not know the meaning of, look at the words around it. Context clues, or the nearby words and sentences, can help you find the meaning of an unfamiliar word. Writers often give an example, a synonym, or an explanation of a word to help you understand words you haven't seen before.

Practice   Read "Home Tweet Home" on page 285. Watch for this week's Words to Know and any other unfamiliar words. Look for context clues to help you understand the meanings of any words you do not know.

Words to Know	bill	hunters	platform
	twigs	material	goo
	tons		

On Your Own   Reread "Home Tweet Home." Make a list of the Words to Know and any unfamiliar words. Then write the words in alphabetical order. Beside each word, write the context clue that helped you understand its meaning. If you need more help, use a dictionary or your glossary.

🐻 **R1.6** Use sentence and word context to find the meaning of unknown words.

Home Tweet Home

A homing pigeon is a kind of bird. It may look like other kinds of birds—with wings, a bill or beak, and feathers—but it can do something very special. A homing pigeon can find its way home from a drop-off point very far away.

Once in a while a homing pigeon does get lost. Hunters may shoot at them, or they might get caught in a bad storm. But most of the time, homing pigeons know just where to go.

Many people like to train homing pigeons. They keep their birds in their yard or on top of a roof. They may build a home with a platform where the birds can take off and land. Inside the home, the birds sleep on grass, twigs, and other kinds of material. The people must keep the pigeon's home clean, free of dirt and other kinds of goo.

Did you know that pigeons can be used to send messages? In France there is a statue in honor of the pigeons used during World War I. It is a large statue that weighs several tons. It shows that pigeons carried messages that helped save the lives of many people.

Need a Review?
See *Words!*, p. W•7 for more information about using context clues to find the meanings of unfamiliar words.

 Ready to Try It?
Read *Amazing Bird Nests*, pp. 288–299.

Build Comprehension

Learn ⊙ **Skill Classify and Categorize**

- To *classify and categorize* means to put things that are related into groups.

- For example, the words in the chart are sorted into two groups. Each group has a label that tells how the words are sorted.

Shapes	Animals
triangle	cow
square	dog
circle	cat

Practice   Read "Do All Birds Fly?" on page 287. As you read, write the names of the different birds mentioned. Think about how they are alike.

On Your Own   **Write to Read** Reread "Do All Birds Fly?" and look at your list of birds. Make a graphic organizer like the one above. Label one column "Birds that fly." and label the other "Birds that do not fly." Classify and categorize the birds by writing the names under the correct label.

 Need a Review? See *Picture It!*, p. PI•4 for more information about classifying and categorizing.

 Ready to Try It? As you read *Amazing Bird Nests*, pp. 288–299, think about how you could classify the nests.

R2.2 Ask questions and support answers by connecting prior knowledge with literal information found in, and inferred, from the text.

Do All Birds Fly?

There are many different kinds of birds in the world. But all birds are alike in some ways. All birds lay eggs. All birds have feathers. And all birds have wings.

Just because all birds have wings, this does not mean that all birds can fly. Penguins are birds but they do not fly. They spend much of their time in water. Penguins use their wings to swim. Penguins are not the only birds that do not fly. Some large birds, like the ostrich, do not fly. They move about only by walking.

Some birds fly but hardly ever walk. The frigate is a bird that does not walk very well. It also does not swim. It gets from place to place only by flying.

Most birds, however, combine flying with some kind of walking or swimming. Look at ducks. They can do three things. They can fly, walk, and swim. Perhaps that is why we sometimes say, "What a lucky duck!"

Skill This paragraph names two kinds of birds that do not fly. You could put them together in a group.

Skill Here is another kind of bird, a frigate. It does fly, so you need to put it in a different group.

Smart Solutions

287

Amazing Bird Nests

by Ron Fridell

Why are these bird nests so amazing?

289

Robin feeding worm to chicks.

A Safe Spot

Look up at the sky. A bird swoops low and lands on a tree branch.

It is spring, the season when birds build nests and lay eggs. The bird hops into its nest and sits gently on the eggs. The nest is their safe spot. It shelters the eggs from wind and rain. It also protects them from snakes, raccoons, and other hungry predators.

After the eggs hatch, the chicks no longer have the shell to protect them. Now the nest helps keep them warm and safe from harm. The parents feed the chicks until they grow bigger and stronger. Then everyone flies away, leaving an empty nest.

Gray Rat Snake raiding a bird's nest.

A Bald Eagle nest built in a tree.

A Hummingbird nest built on a pinecone.

Very Small and Very Big

Some birds build very small nests. Hummingbird nests are smallest of all. Some are just an inch across and an inch deep. Talk about small spaces! When the tiny female hummingbird sits on the eggs, her head sticks out one end of the nest and her tail out the other.

Some birds build very big nests. The nest of the American Bald Eagle can be ten feet across and twenty feet deep. It can weigh as much as two tons. That's more than most cars weigh! Eagles build their huge nests way high up at the tops of trees and mountains. That makes sense. Eagles are birds of prey. They are hunters. They spend their time high in the air, looking down for their next tasty meal.

All Kinds of Shapes

Birds should be proud of their nests. Each kind of bird builds its own special type of nest. Hummingbirds build little nests shaped like cups. Eagles build big, flat, platform nests. Woodpeckers build cavity nests by pecking holes in trees.

Which bird should win the prize for best nest-builder? How about the weaver bird? It uses its sharp bill like a needle to sew strips of fresh grass together. Then it weaves them into a nest. Weaver birds use a dozen kinds of knots to build their amazing home. It takes them about 500 trips to cut down and carry back all the grass to do the job.

A Sociable Weaver nest colony in a Quiver tree.

Ruppell's Weaver building a nest.

Gila Woodpecker at nest in a Saguaro cactus.

Kittiwakes nesting on the side of a bridge.

All Kinds of Places

Birds live in forests, deserts, grasslands, and wetlands. They live in the country and the city.

As cities take the place of forests and fields, birds must adapt to changing environments. City birds must build their nests in new and unusual places. Some use telephone poles, street lights, and mailboxes. Others build their nests in unused chimneys, flowerpots, and empty cans. Sometimes these city nests get in our way.

Watch Them Grow

Let's say a bird starts building a nest on the ledge outside your window. You could chase it away. Or, better, you could welcome the bird and watch it do its amazing work. Most birds take a week or two to build a nest.

Most bird eggs hatch in about three weeks. Baby birds usually spend another couple of weeks living in the nest. Watch them and you will see how the parents feed and care for their chicks. Keep watching as your bird family grows up and, finally, flies away.

One-day-old chicks

All Kinds of Stuff

It's amazing how much strange stuff birds use to build their nests. Some birds use old snake skin in their nests. Some birds use sticky spider silk to hold things together. To make the inside of the nest soft and warm, some birds use animal hair. Others line their nests with more than a thousand feathers!

Great Grey Bowerbird decorating its bower, or nest.

Raven chicks in nest built from barbed wire, plastic, garbage, and bones.

Swiftlets in nests with eggs.

Even More Stuff

City birds have lots of different materials to choose from. In some city nests you will find bits of paper and plastic wrap. In others you'll see paper clips, thumbtacks, hairpins, rubber bands, and barbed wire. One person even found money tucked away in a bird's nest—a five-dollar bill!

Bird's nest soup!

The Strangest Nest

The strangest nest of all may be the white-nest swiftlet's. A swiftlet is a small bird that lives in Asian nations such as India and Thailand. What makes this bird's nest so strange?

A swiftlet nest is made of a goo that comes from the bird's mouth. That's right, the swiftlet spits out its nest! The goo comes out looking like long, wet noodles. The bird takes about a month to weave this sticky stuff into a cup-shaped nest. Soon, the goo dries out and becomes strong and sturdy.

Some people make soup from these nests. They really do! Workers use rope ladders to collect them from cliffs and cave roofs. Then cooks make it into soup and serve it in restaurants.

Why would people eat bird's nest soup? They believe that swiftlet goo will make them look and feel younger and healthier.

Amazing Birds

How do birds learn how to build these strange and amazing nests? Who teaches them?

No one. When a bird builds a nest for the first time, it has never seen one made before. The bird does not have to think about what it is doing. It just "knows" what to do. Just like you and I know how to breathe.

Ovenbird building a nest from mud and grass.

Atlantic Puffin collecting sticks and grass for a nest.

Northern Gannet using seaweed and algae to build nest.

But that doesn't mean that building a nest is an easy job. Far from it. Think about the 500 trips a weaver bird must make to bring back the grass to build its nest. Or the dozen different kinds of knots it uses to weave it.

And remember that birds must do nearly the whole job with their beak, along with a little help from their feet. That would be like you using only a finger and thumb on one hand.

Try building a nest some time from a pile of thin twigs, roots, and grass. Birds are amazing animals, and they build amazing homes.

Think, Talk and Write

Talk About It The section called "The Strangest Nest" on page 297 gives some facts about a very unusual kind of nest. Tell your ideas about this strange nest.

1. Use the pictures below to summarize what you learned. **Summarize**

2. Which of these things does not belong in this group: grass, bricks, goo, old snake skin? How could you label the group? **Classify and Categorize**

3. The author uses a compare-and-contrast structure to organize the information on page 291. How does the structure help you understand what you read? **Text Structure**

4. Use words from the Words to Know list on p. 284 and from the selection to write three sentences about the American Bald Eagle's nest. **Vocabulary**

Look Back and Write Look back at the question on page 289. You have read about several kinds of bird nests. Choose one that you find interesting. Write a paragraph telling what makes that nest amazing. Be sure to include details from the article to support your answer.

Meet author Ron Fridell on page 448.

Summarize

G4R2.1 Identify structural patterns found in informational text (e.g., compare and contrast, cause and effect, sequential or chronological order, proposition and support) to strengthen comprehension.

Writing | Description

Prompt *Amazing Bird Nests* tells how birds solve problems in their environment. Think about the kinds of bird nests you have seen. Now write a description of one of those nests.

Writing Trait

Word choice includes strong adjectives, nouns, and verbs.

Student Model

Hidden Nest

Once I saw two quail nests. They were at the edge of a large grassy field. I was hiking with my dad when he showed me the first one. It was under a blackberry patch.

The dirt was pressed down to make a bowl shape. Inside the birds had put dry grass, pine needles, feathers, and dead leaves. The inside of the nest had turned purple from falling blackberries.

My dad said quail usually live in a group called a covey. He said we should look for other nests. It took a little while, but I found the second one. The birds' nests were well hidden!

Strong word choice makes writing clear and interesting to read.

Plural possessive nouns end with an apostrophe.

A description elaborates with strong details.

Use the model to help you write your own description.

W2.2 Write descriptions that use concrete sensory details to present and support unified impressions of people, places, things, or experiences.

301

Smart Solutions

Main Idea and Details is one kind of text structure. Authors often use this text structure when they need to organize a lot of information about one topic. Section headings help readers to find the main ideas in a long piece of text.

Ready to Try It?
Read *A Journey into Adaptation*. Look for the main idea and supporting details in each section of the text.

Science Link

This selection describes some animals that have adapted to their environments. Use the library or the Internet to research a plant that has adapted to its habitat. Draw and label a picture that shows the adaptation.

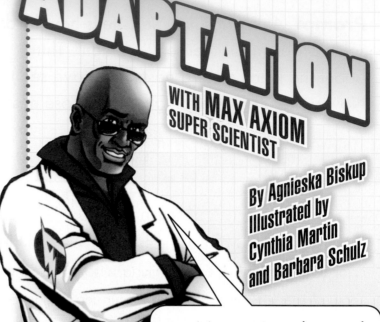

A JOURNEY INTO
ADAPTATION

WITH **MAX AXIOM**
SUPER SCIENTIST

By Agnieska Biskup
Illustrated by
Cynthia Martin
and Barbara Schulz

Most animals need many generations to adapt to their environments. Rapid changes in an environment make survival very difficult.

Why did the dinosaurs go extinct? No one knows for sure. But some scientists believe that the climate changed quickly after a meteorite the size of a mountain hit Earth.

The meteorite's impact threw huge amounts of dust and ash into the air. This debris blocked out the sun's light and temperatures fell.

With less sunlight and colder temperatures, plants began to die. The dinosaurs that ate those plants now had less to eat. As the plant-eating dinosaurs died, the meat-eaters also lost their food source.

The dinosaurs couldn't adapt to these sudden changes and died. Clearly, being able to adapt really is a matter of life and death.

The body features, or physical adaptations, of plants and animals often relate to the environments they live in.

For example, a camel's hump is an adaptation for desert life. When food and water are scarce, the camel uses fat stored in its hump for energy.

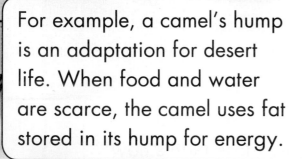

The camel's long eyelashes protect its eyes from blowing sand.

CREOSOTE BUSH

BARREL CACTUS

Plants also cope with dry desert conditions. Since plants lose water through their leaves, the creosote bush's leaves have a waxy coating to help the plant hold in water. In many cases, plants lack leaves altogether. The barrel cactus stores water in its fleshy stem.

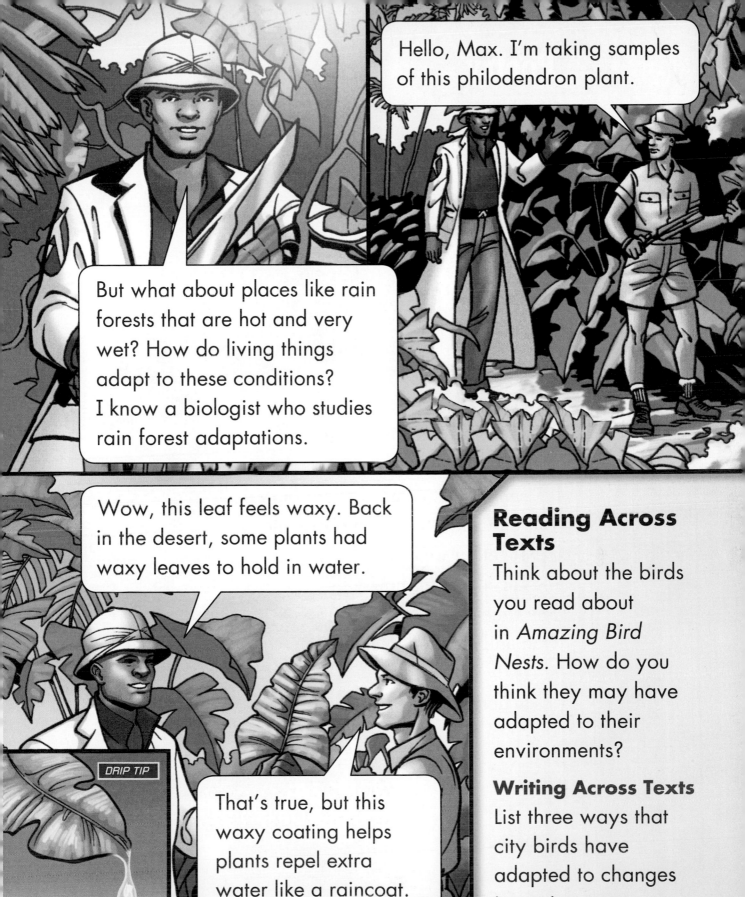

Hello, Max. I'm taking samples of this philodendron plant.

But what about places like rain forests that are hot and very wet? How do living things adapt to these conditions? I know a biologist who studies rain forest adaptations.

Wow, this leaf feels waxy. Back in the desert, some plants had waxy leaves to hold in water.

DRIP TIP

That's true, but this waxy coating helps plants repel extra water like a raincoat.

Reading Across Texts
Think about the birds you read about in *Amazing Bird Nests*. How do you think they may have adapted to their environments?

Writing Across Texts
List three ways that city birds have adapted to changes in environment.

305

Ants

by Marilyn Singer

One and one and one and one
    Dead leaves
    Dead crickets
One ant alone can't pick it
    up
    can't drag this meal to our busy nest
But one and one and one and one
    Together we tow
    Together we know
any time of day this is so:
One and one and one and one
    is the best way
    to get things done

The Sure-Footed Shoe Finder

by Andrea Perry

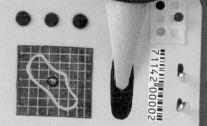

How many times has this happened to you?
You're late for the school bus and can't find a shoe.
It might take you hours unless you have got
The Sure-Footed Shoe Finder there on the spot!

Just lift up the lever and open the gate,
then toss in the shoe that is missing its mate.
With a beep and a clang and a stagger and lurch,
the Shoe Finder's off on its shoe-finding search.

The powerful Foot-Odor-Sensitive Vent
tracks down your sneaker by matching its scent,
and mere seconds later the shoe is retrieved.
You won't miss the school bus! Now aren't
you relieved?

Most of our customers happen to choose
our standard shoe model for footwear they lose,
although the new jumbo Shoe Finder can trace
even those snow boots you children misplace!

Third-Grade GENIUS

by Gary Soto

Me, I took two wires, a battery, and a bulb
And fit them nicely together in my hand.

Show and tell.

I said, "I know about electricity."
Then I walked up and down the aisles,
    showing my invention,
A flashlight of sorts. This on a rainy day,
With the battery of the sun gone dead.
This on a day when the headlights of cars
    came on at noon.

Me, I showed my friends about electricity,
The beam of my invention glinting off the
    teacher's glasses.
I beamed it at the hamster, whose eyes glowed
    red as berries.

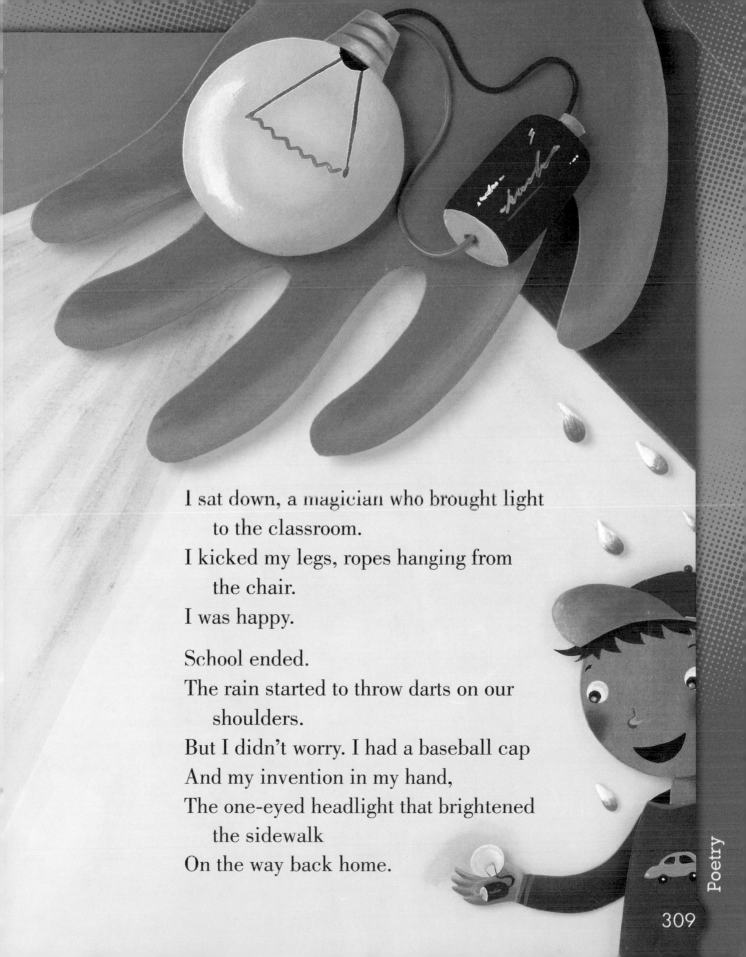

I sat down, a magician who brought light
   to the classroom.
I kicked my legs, ropes hanging from
   the chair.
I was happy.

School ended.
The rain started to throw darts on our
   shoulders.
But I didn't worry. I had a baseball cap
And my invention in my hand,
The one-eyed headlight that brightened
   the sidewalk
On the way back home.

Get Online!

PearsonSuccessNet.com

See It!
- Concept Talk Video
- *Picture It!* Animation
- e-Books

Hear It!
- Selection Snapshot and Response
- Paired Selection e-Text
- Grammar Jammer
- e-Books

Do It!
- Online Journal
- Story Sort
- New Literacies Activity
- Success Tracker

People and Nature

THE BIG **?**

How are people and nature connected?

People and Nature

Let's Talk About
Enjoying Nature

LS1.7 Use clear and specific vocabulary to communicate ideas and establish the tone.

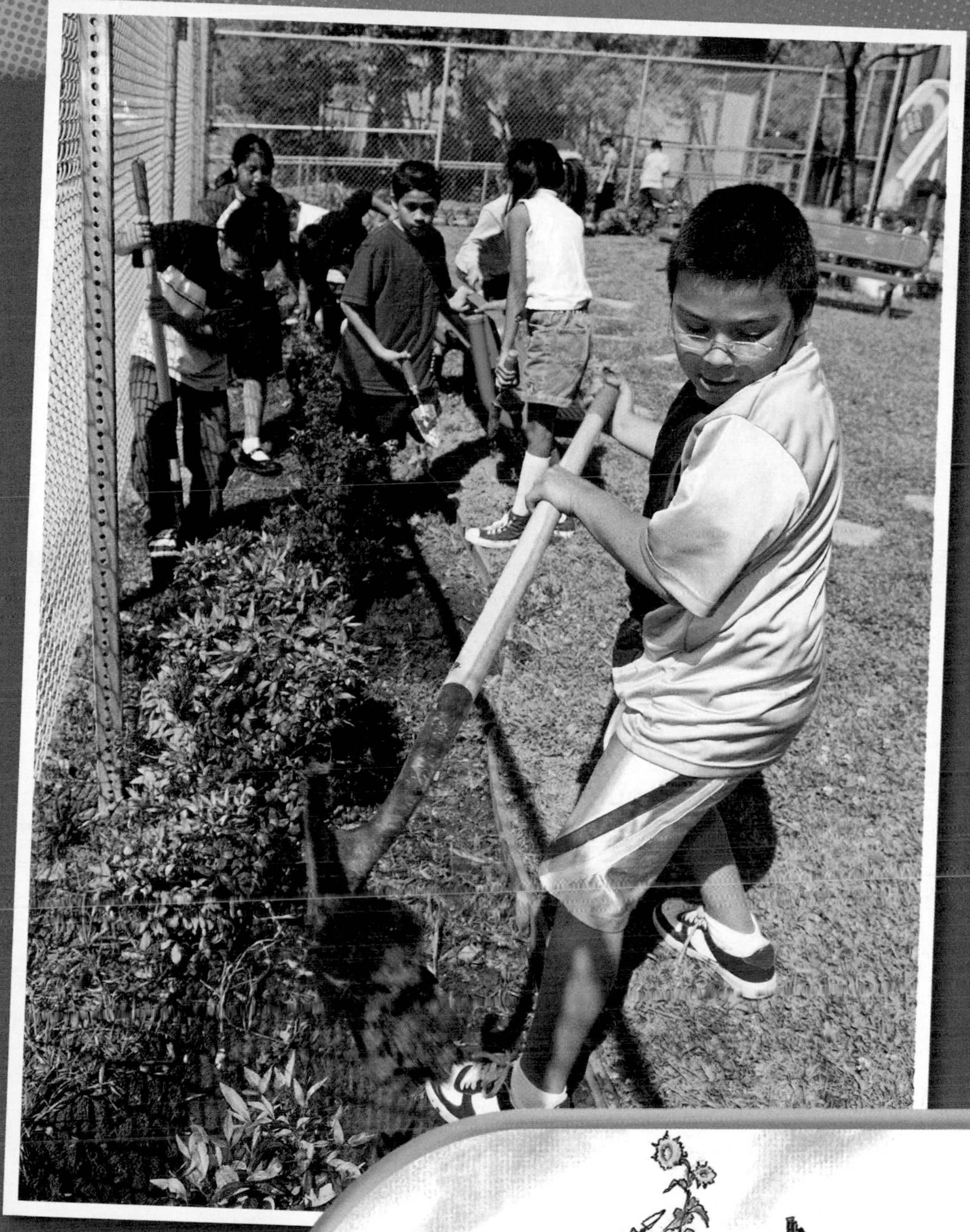

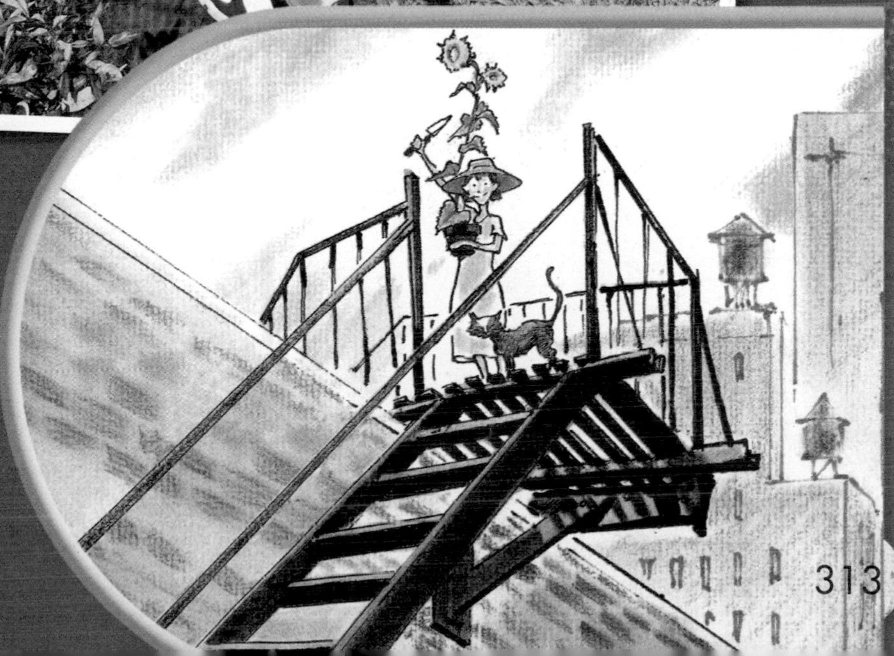

Build Vocabulary

Learn ⊙ **Skill Homophones** are words that sound the same but have different meanings and spellings, such as *write* (meaning "to form letters or words") and *right* (meaning "correct"). Context clues can help you figure out which meaning goes with which spelling of a homophone. Remember, context clues are the words and sentences around the confusing word.

Practice Read "Bulbs to Blooms" on page 315. Look for words that may be homophones.

Words to Know	bulbs	sprouting	showers
	blooming	recognizing	beauty
	humor	knead	doze

On Your Own Reread "Bulbs to Blooms." Find at least three words that have homophones. For each word, write its homophone and the meanings of both words.

R1.4 Use knowledge of antonyms, synonyms, homophones, and homographs to determine the meanings of words. **R1.6** Use sentence and word context to find the meaning of unknown words.

Bulbs to Blooms

Every fall Mr. Connor plants bulbs in his yard. The bulbs look like big, ugly brown lumps. It's hard to imagine them sprouting roots and stems and becoming plants. Yet, after a few early spring rain showers, dozens of tulips and daffodils will be blooming in Mr. Connor's yard. It is a wonderful sight. Mr. Connor has won awards recognizing his yard for its beauty. He is very proud of his bulbs. Fortunately, he also has a sense of humor.

One day last fall, I was making bread in the kitchen. As I stood at the counter to knead the dough, I could look out the window and watch Mr. Connor watering his yard. Then I left the dough to rise and went to sit on the porch with my dog Champ. Soon I started to doze.

When I woke up, Champ was in Mr. Connor's yard, digging up the bulbs! I was horrified, but Mr. Connor just laughed. He said he could have used a good hole digger. Then I helped him replant the bulbs.

Need a Review?
See *Words!*, p. W•12 for more information about homophones.

Ready to Try It?
Read *The Gardener*, pp. 318–331.

Build Comprehension

Learn **Skill Cause and Effect**

- A cause tells *why* something happened.

- An effect is *what* happened.

- Clue words like *because* and *so* can help you find the cause and its effect.

- Sometimes a cause has more than one effect.

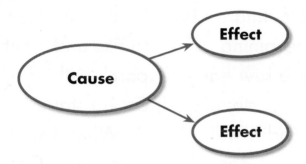

Practice   Read "Winter Blooms" on page 317. Look for clue words to help you find cause-and-effect relationships.

On Your Own   **Write to Read** Reread "Winter Blooms" and make a graphic organizer like the one above. Try to find a cause that has more than one effect. Then use your graphic organizer to write a paragraph that explains three effects of Margo reading the book. Use clue words in your paragraph.

❚❚ Need a Review?
See *Picture It!*, p. PI•3 for more information about cause and effect.

▶ Ready to Try It?
As you read *The Gardener*, pp. 318–331, look for cause-and-effect relationships.

  G2R2.6 Recognize cause-and-effect relationships in a text.

Winter Blooms

Margo loved flowers. They made her think of spring. There were no flowers growing in the yard now because it was January and the ground was frozen. Margo wondered how to grow flowers in her house, so she went to the library for a book.

She read the book carefully so she would know how to make flowers grow in her house. The book had a list of what she needed for an indoor garden, so she went to the garden shop to buy some supplies. The book said flowers grow best near a window because they needed plenty of sun. So, she set her new green plants on her kitchen windowsill. The book also said that flowers need water. Margo put the watering can near the sink to remind her to water the plants often. She looked at her dreary yard and then at her cheerful pots of plants. She hoped they would bloom soon!

Skill There are some clue words in this paragraph— *because* and *so*. What causes and effects can you find in this paragraph?

Skill Here's an example of a cause that has two effects. Ask yourself, "Why did Margo's book say to put plants near a window?" This question will help you figure out the cause and its other effect.

People and Nature

317

The Gardener

by Sarah Stewart
illustrated by David Small

Genre

Realistic fiction is a made-up story that could happen in real life. What parts of this selection could really happen?

Who is this gardener, and what does she do that is special?

August 27, 1935

Dear Uncle Jim,

Grandma told us after supper that you want me to come to the city and live with you until things get better. Did she tell you that Papa has been out of work for a long time, and no one asks Mama to make dresses anymore?

We all cried, even Papa. But then Mama made us laugh with her stories about your chasing her up trees when you were both little. Did you really do that?

I'm small, but strong, and I'll help you all I can. However, Grandma said to finish my schoolwork before doing anything else.

Your niece,
Lydia Grace Finch

September 3, 1935

Dear Uncle Jim,

I'm mailing this from the train station. I forgot to tell you in the last letter *three important things* that I'm too shy to say to your face:

1. I know a lot about gardening, but nothing about baking.

2. I'm anxious to learn to bake, but is there any place to plant seeds?

3. I like to be called "Lydia Grace"—just like Grandma.

Your niece,
Lydia Grace Finch

On the train
September 4, 1935
Dear Mama,

   I feel so pretty in your dress that you made over for me. I hope you don't miss it too much.

Dear Papa,

   I haven't forgotten what you said about recognizing Uncle Jim: "Just look for Mama's face with a big nose and a mustache!" I promise not to tell him. (Does he have a sense of humor?)

And, dearest Grandma,

   Thank you for the seeds. The train is rocking me to sleep, and every time I doze off, I dream of gardens.
                    Love to all,
                    Lydia Grace

September 5, 1935
Dear Mama, Papa, and Grandma,
    I'm so excited!!!
    There are window boxes here! They look as if they've been waiting for me, so now we'll both wait for spring.
    And, Grandma, the sun shines down on the corner where I'll live and work.
        Love to all,
        Lydia Grace
P.S. Uncle Jim doesn't smile.

December 25, 1935
Dear Mama, Papa, and Grandma,

I adore the seed catalogues you sent for Christmas. And, Grandma, thank you for all the bulbs. I hope you received my drawings.

I wrote a long poem for Uncle Jim. He didn't smile, but I think he liked it. He read it aloud, then put it in his shirt pocket and patted it.

Love to all,
Lydia Grace

February 12, 1936

Dearest Grandma,

Thank you again for those bulbs you sent at Christmas. You should see them now!

I really like Ed and Emma Beech, Uncle Jim's friends who work here. When I first arrived, Emma told me she'd show me how to knead bread if I would teach her the Latin names of all the flowers I know. Now, just half a year later, I'm kneading bread and she's speaking Latin!

More good news: We have a store cat named Otis who at this very moment is sleeping at the foot of *my* bed.

Love to all,

Lydia Grace

P.S. Uncle Jim isn't smiling yet, but I'm hoping for a smile soon.

March 5, 1936
Dear Mama, Papa, and Grandma,
    I've discovered a secret place. You can't imagine how wonderful it is. No one else knows about it but Otis.
    I have great plans.
    Thank you for all the letters. I'll try to write more, but I'm really busy planting all your seeds in cracked teacups and bent cake pans! And, Grandma, you should smell the good dirt I'm bringing home from the vacant lot down the street.
                    Love to all,
                    Lydia Grace

April 27, 1936

Dearest Grandma,

All the seeds and roots are sprouting. I can hear you saying, "April showers bring May flowers."

Emma and I are sprucing up the bakery and I'm playing a great trick on Uncle Jim. He sees me reading my mail, planting seeds in the window boxes, going to school, doing my homework, sweeping the floor. But he never sees me working in my secret place.

Love to all,
Lydia Grace
P.S. I'm planning on a big smile from Uncle Jim in the near future.

May 27, 1936

Dear Mama, Papa, and Grandma,

You should have heard Emma laugh today when I opened your letter and dirt fell out onto the sidewalk! Thank you for all the baby plants. They survived the trip in the big envelope.

More about Emma: She's helping me with the secret place. Hurrah!

Love to all,
Lydia Grace

P.S. I saw Uncle Jim almost smile today. The store was full (well, *almost* full) of customers.

June 27, 1936

Dear Grandma,

    Flowers are blooming all over the place. I'm also growing radishes, onions, and three kinds of lettuce in the window boxes.

    Some neighbors have brought containers for me to fill with flowers, and a few customers even gave me plants from their gardens this spring! They don't call me "Lydia Grace" anymore. They call me "the gardener."

            Love to all,

            Lydia Grace

    P.S. I'm sure Uncle Jim will smile soon. I'm almost ready to show him the secret place.

July 4, 1936

Dearest Mama, Papa, and Grandma,

I am bursting with happiness! The entire city seems so beautiful, especially this morning.

The secret place is ready for Uncle Jim. At noon, the store will close for the holiday, and then we'll bring him up to the roof.

I've tried to remember everything you ever taught me about beauty.

Love to all,
Lydia Grace

P.S. I can already imagine Uncle Jim's smile.

July 11, 1936

Dear Mama, Papa, and Grandma,

My heart is pounding so hard I'm sure the customers can hear it downstairs!

At lunch today, Uncle Jim put the "Closed" sign on the door and told Ed and Emma and me to go upstairs and wait. He appeared with the most amazing cake I've ever seen—covered in flowers!

I truly believe that cake equals one thousand smiles.

And then he took your letter out of his pocket with the news of Papa's job!

I'M COMING HOME!

Love to all, and see you soon,
Lydia Grace

P.S. Grandma, I've given all of my plants to Emma. I can't wait to help you in your garden again. We gardeners never retire.

Think, Talk and Write

Talk About It Lydia Grace certainly makes the best of things. Some people would say that when life handed her a lemon, she made lemonade. Tell some ways in which Lydia Grace shows she is that kind of person.

1. Use the pictures below to retell the story. **Retell**

2. What effect did Lydia Grace's visit have on Uncle Jim? Why do you think so? **Cause and Effect**

3. What was Lydia Grace trying to achieve when she first arrived at Uncle Jim's? By the end of the story, did she succeed? **Story Structure**

4. Uncle Jim's customers began calling Lydia Grace "the gardener." Explain this new name. Use words from the Words to Know list on p. 314. **Vocabulary**

TEST PRACTICE

Look Back and Write Look back at the question on page 319. Think about how Lydia Grace makes her special garden. Now that you've read *The Gardener,* write a response to the question. Be sure to include details from the story to support your answer.

Meet author **Sarah Stewart on page 451 and** illustrator **David Small on page 450.**

Retell

G2R2.6 Recognize cause-and-effect relationships in a text. **G4R3.2** Identify the main events of the plot, their causes, and the influence of each event on future actions.

Writing   Realistic Story

Prompt *The Gardener* is a narrative that tells a realistic story about a girl and her garden. Imagine a place in nature that you enjoy. Now write a realistic story that takes place in that setting.

Student Model

Anna's Quiet Place

Anna had a big family. Her two brothers and three sisters kept the house jumping with noise and activity. Anna dreamed of a quiet place where she could read and write. Anna's neighbor, Mrs. Burton, understood Anna's problem. Mrs. Burton came up with a plan and Anna's mother agreed.

The next afternoon Mrs. Burton took Anna to her lush backyard. The giant oak tree there held a secret hiding place – a wonderful little tree house set securely in the space between two strong limbs. Mrs. Burton pointed and said, "Anna, this tree house is yours to hide out in whenever you need peace and quiet. Just be sure to let your mother know when you're coming."

Anna was very happy. When she visited the tree house the next day, she read *The Giving Tree* by Shel Silverstein. Then she wrote a story about what her new tree meant to her.

This is the most important idea of the story. The other sentences all support this idea.

Linking verbs link the subject to the predicate.

Realistic fiction happens in a setting that seems real.

Use the model to help you write your own realistic story.

W2.1b Write narratives: Include well-chosen details to develop the plot.

People and Nature

333

▶ **Ready to Try It?**
As you read "Worms at Work," look at the text features. How do the numbered steps, headings, and photos help you as you read?

Science Link

Use reference materials to find out more about an earthworm's body. Draw and label a picture of one.

Worms at Work

by Ann Weil

Did you know that people all over the world keep worms to change their garbage into rich soil called *compost?* Worms eat food scraps. Two pounds of worms can eat a pound of garbage every day. That's a lot of trash.

Keeping worms is easy. It can also be a lot of fun. And while you're having fun taking care of the worms, you're also helping our environment by recycling trash into compost for houseplants and gardens.

Here's what you need to do.

You will need:

- Red worms ·····················○
  (also called red wigglers)

  > You can start with as few as **50–100** worms, but more worms will eat more garbage. Some garden stores sell worms by the pound. One pound of worms contains **1,000–1,500** worms.

- A large plastic container, about 12 inches deep

  12"

- Plastic bag or loose cover for the container

- Newspaper, leaves, and soil to make the bedding

  ## Feeding Dos

  YES: Eggshells; coffee grounds and used tea bags; cooked rice, pasta, or potatoes; cereals; fruit and vegetable peelings; bread

- Water

  ## Feeding Don'ts

  NO: Meat and fish, dairy products. Worms would eat these, but they may make the worm bin smell bad and attract rats and flies.

- Food scraps ·····················○

Making Your Worm Bin

1 **Prepare the container.**
Poke small holes through the bottom of the container.

2 **Prepare the bedding.** ·········○
Fill the container about three-quarters full with small pieces of torn newspaper. (Do not use any colored or shiny newspaper.)

Add about a handful of soil. You can put in some dead leaves, too, if you like.

3 **Pour water on the bedding.** ·····················○
Make sure all the bedding is damp, but not soaking wet.

4 **Add the worms.**
Gently move the worms into their new home.

5 **Feed the worms.** ············○
Bury the food scraps in the bedding.

6 **Cover the bin.**
Make sure air can still move in and around the bin.

Maintaining Your Worm Bin

1 Keep the bedding moist.
Make sure the bedding does not dry out.

2 Feed the worms. ·············O
Pay attention to how much the worms are eating. If they are not eating all the scraps, feed them less.

3 Harvest the compost. ·············O
Worms eat their bedding as well as their food. When the bedding is mostly gone, push what's left to one side and add fresh, damp bedding to the other side. Bury the food scraps in the new bedding. The worms will move to the food so you can harvest the compost without taking all the worms with it.

4 Use the compost!
Compost helps plants grow better. Add it to potted houseplants or to your outdoor flower or vegetable garden.

Reading Across Texts
You have read *The Gardener* and "Worms at Work." What do both selections tell about taking care of a garden?

Writing Across Texts
Make a list of helpful things that worms do for us.

Let's Talk About
Explaining Nature

LS1.7 Use clear and specific vocabulary to communicate ideas and establish the tone.

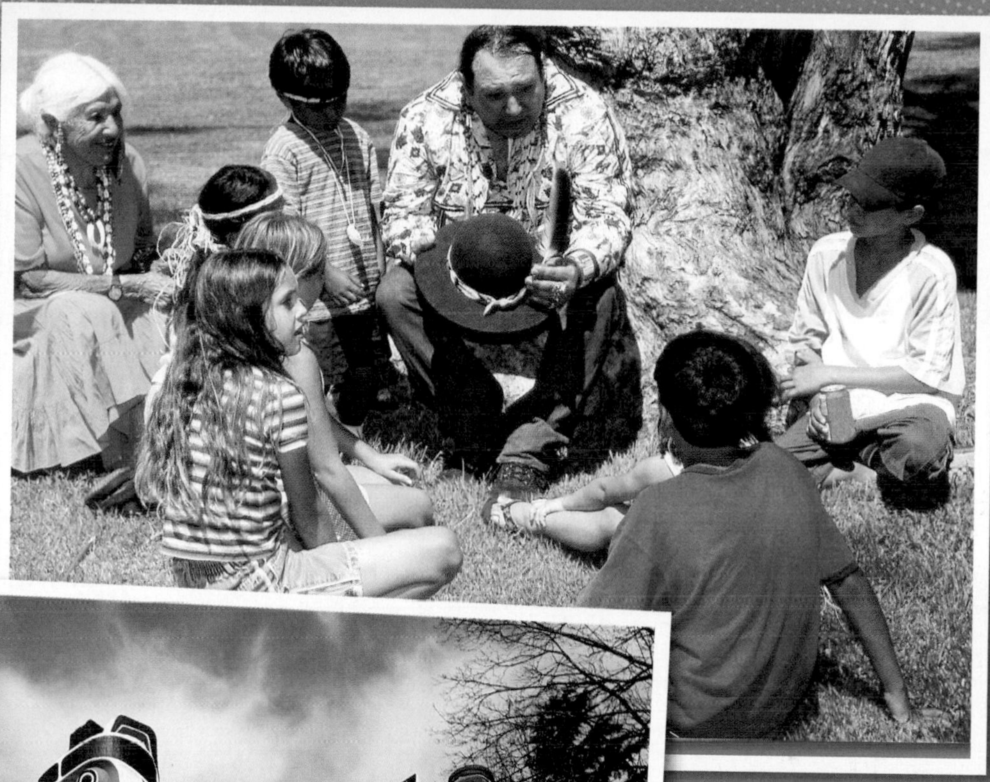

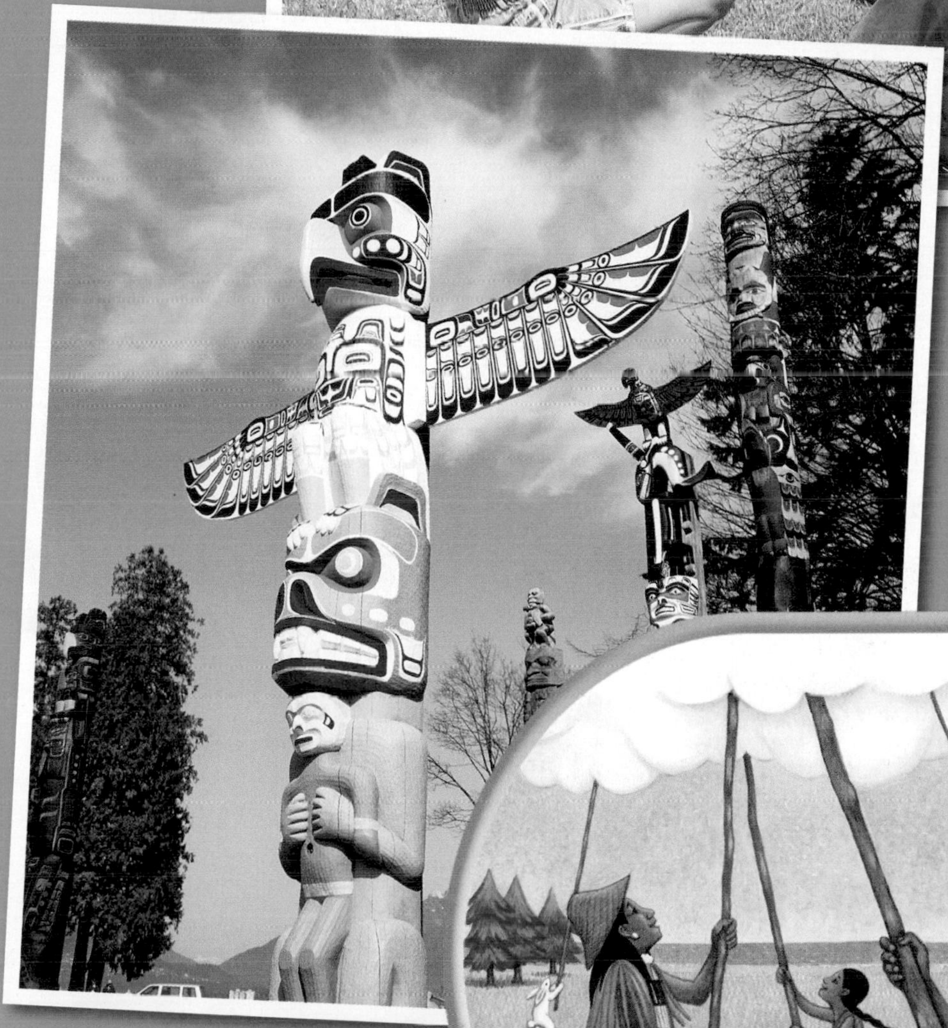

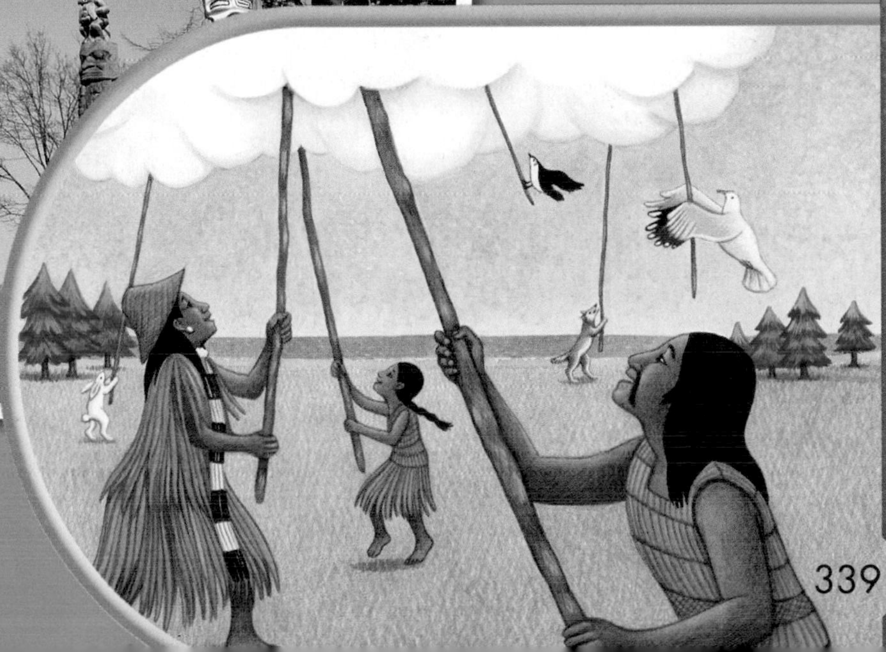

Build Vocabulary

Learn ⊙ **Skill Unfamiliar Words** If you don't know the meaning of a word in your reading, you can look it up in a dictionary or the glossary at the back of this book. Some words listed in the dictionary will have more than one definition. If the word has more than one meaning, decide which meaning you think fits in the sentence.

Practice Read "The Class Play" on page 341. As you read, make a list of the highlighted words. Use the glossary at the back of this book or a dictionary to find the meaning of each word. Write the meaning next to each word on your list.

Words to Know	overhead	poked	imagined
	narrator	antlers	languages

On Your Own Reread "The Class Play." Imagine that you are Ms. Chavez. What would you say to Jenna and Kate? Write your response. Use as many words from the Words to Know list as you can.

340 **R1.7** Use a dictionary to learn the meaning and other features of unknown words. **R2.1** Use titles, tables of contents, chapter headings, glossaries, and indexes to locate information in text.

The Class Play

"I have counted the votes," declared Ms. Chavez, waving a sheet of paper overhead. "Our play for Parents Night will be *Pushing Up the Sky*. Tryouts are tomorrow."

Jenna grinned and poked Kate in the shoulder. They both wanted to be Chiefs together. They had already learned the lines and planned their costumes.

The next day Jenna tried out for the First Chief. That was scarier than she had imagined. She forgot several words.

When Kate tried out for the Seventh Chief's part, she didn't make a single mistake.

Later, Ms. Chavez announced the parts. Kate was the Narrator. She had a lot of lines, but she didn't get to wear a costume. "But I made a beautiful cape," she wailed.

Jenna was the Elk. She didn't have any lines at all, and she had to wear brown paper antlers on her head. "Don't elks know *any* languages?"

Both girls were disappointed but glad to be in the play. Maybe next time they will get the parts they want.

 Need a Review?
See *Words!*, p. W•14 for more information about using a glossary or dictionary.

 Ready to Try It?
Read *Pushing Up the Sky*, pp. 344–355.

People and Nature

Build Comprehension

Learn   ⊙ **Skill Compare and Contrast**

- When you make a comparison, you tell how two or more things are alike and how they are different.

- When you make a contrast, you tell only how things are different.

- A Venn diagram is a useful tool for comparing and contrasting.

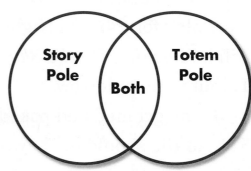

Story Pole   Both   Totem Pole

Practice   Read "An Up-and-Down Story" on page 343. Look for ways in which a story pole and a totem pole are alike and different.

On Your Own   **Write to Read** Reread "An Up-and-Down Story." Make a Venn diagram to compare and contrast the two kinds of poles described in the passage. Then write a paragraph explaining how the poles are alike and different.

❚❚ Need a Review?
See *Picture It!*, p. PI•5 for more practice with comparing and contrasting.

▶ Ready to Try It?
As you read *Pushing Up the Sky*, pp. 344–355, watch for comparisons and contrasts.

342   **G4R2.1** Identify structural patterns found in informational text (e.g., compare and contrast, cause and effect, sequential or chronological order, proposition and support) to strengthen comprehension.

An Up -and- Down Story

One of the world's tallest totem poles stands in Kalama, Washington, on the banks of the Columbia River. Carved from a Western Red Cedar tree, the totem pole is 140 feet tall. The tall Kalama totem pole is decorated with symbols. These symbols are part of the culture of Native Americans of the Pacific Northwest.

In nearby Olympia, Washington, you will find another tall pole. However, this pole is not a totem pole. It is a story pole. A story pole is different from a totem pole. A totem pole tells about a family. A story pole uses animal stories to teach children about their culture and responsibility. The story pole in Olympia has 21 carved figures on it. Each teaches a lesson about life.

Both poles were carved by Native American artists. Chief Don Lelooska carved the Kalama totem pole. Chief Lelooska was born into the Cherokee tribe and learned the carving style of the Kwakiutl people. The Olympia story pole was carved by Chief William Shelton of the Snohomish tribe.

Skill This paragraph describes a totem pole. The next paragraph will describe a story pole. What is different about the purposes of the poles?

Skill Here is a clue word that tells you this paragraph will be about how the two kinds of poles are alike.

Pushing Up

by Joseph Bruchac

illustrated by Teresa Flavin

A **play** uses a cast of characters. Look at the characters in *Pushing Up the Sky* and think about which role you would like to play.

the Sky

What would happen if you could touch the sky?

Snohomish

The Snohomish people live in the area of the Northwest that is now known as the state of Washington, not far from Puget Sound. They fished in the ocean and gathered food from the shore. Their homes and many of the things they used every day, such as bowls and canoe paddles, were carved from the trees. Like many of the other peoples of the area, they also carved totem poles, which recorded the history and stories of their nation. This story is one that was carved into a totem pole made for the city of Everett, Washington, by Chief William Shelton.

Characters

Speaking Roles

NARRATOR	**FIRST CHIEF**
TALL MAN	**SECOND CHIEF**
GIRL	**THIRD CHIEF**
MOTHER	**FOURTH CHIEF**
BOY	**FIFTH CHIEF**
	SIXTH CHIEF
	SEVENTH CHIEF

Non-speaking Roles

Animals and Birds—as many as group size will accommodate. Animals familiar to the Snohomish would include Dog, Deer, Elk, Mountain Goat, Bear, Mountain Lion, Rabbit, Weasel, Wolf, and Fox. Birds would include Hawk, Bald Eagle, Golden Eagle, Jay, Seagull, Raven, Heron, and Kingfisher.

Props/Scenery

The village can be suggested with a painted backdrop showing houses made of cedar planks among tall fir trees and redwoods, with the ocean visible in the background. Potted plants can be added around the stage to suggest trees if desired.

Bows and arrows held by Boy in Scene I can be from a toy set or made from cardboard.

The poles held by people and animals in Scene III can be rulers or long tubes of cardboard.

Costumes

People, including the **Narrator,** can wear blankets or towels. **Chiefs** wear them around their shoulders, and other humans wear them wrapped around their waists to suggest the robes often worn by people of the Northwest. Cone-shaped hats (worn by Snohomish women) may be worn by girls playing human characters.

Depending on their number and type, the **Animals** can be suggested by face paint or with decorated masks made from paper plates.

Scene I: A Village Among Many Tall Trees

(Tall Man, Girl, Mother, and Boy stand onstage.)

NARRATOR: Long ago the sky was very close to the earth. The sky was so close that some people could jump right into it. Those people who were not good jumpers could climb up the tall fir trees and step into the sky. But people were not happy that the sky was so close to the earth. Tall people kept bumping their heads on the sky. And there were other problems.

TALL MAN: Oh, that hurt! I just hit my head on the sky again.

GIRL: I just threw my ball, and it landed in the sky, and I can't get it back.

MOTHER: Where is my son? Has he climbed a tree and gone up into the sky again?

BOY: Every time I shoot my bow, my arrows get stuck in the sky!

ALL: THE SKY IS TOO CLOSE!

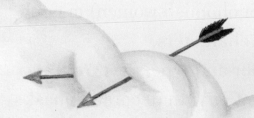

Scene II: The Same Village

(The seven chiefs stand together onstage.)

NARRATOR: So people decided something had to be done. A great meeting was held for all the different tribes. The seven wisest chiefs got together to talk about the problem.

FIRST CHIEF: My people all think the sky is too close.

SECOND CHIEF: The Creator did a very good job of making the world.

THIRD CHIEF: That is true, but the Creator should have put the sky up higher. My tall son keeps hitting his head on the sky.

FOURTH CHIEF: My daughter keeps losing her ball in the sky.

FIFTH CHIEF: People keep going up into the sky when they should be staying on the earth to help each other.

SIXTH CHIEF: When mothers look for their children, they cannot find them because they are up playing in the sky.

SEVENTH CHIEF: We are agreed, then. The sky is too close.

ALL: WE ARE AGREED.

SECOND CHIEF: What can we do?

SEVENTH CHIEF: I have an idea. Let's push up the sky.

THIRD CHIEF: The sky is heavy.

SEVENTH CHIEF: If we all push together, we can do it.

SIXTH CHIEF: We will ask the birds and animals to help. They also do not like it that the sky is so close.

SECOND CHIEF: The elk are always getting their antlers caught in the sky.

FOURTH CHIEF: The birds are always hitting their wings on it.

FIRST CHIEF: We will cut tall trees to make poles. We can use those poles to push up the sky.

FIFTH CHIEF: That is a good idea. Are we all agreed?

ALL: WE ARE ALL AGREED.

Scene III: The Same Village

(All the People, except Seventh Chief, are gathered together. They hold long poles. The Birds and Animals are with them. They all begin pushing randomly, jabbing their poles into the air. The sky can be imagined as just above them.)

GIRL: It isn't working.

BOY: The sky is still too close.

FIFTH CHIEF: Where is Seventh Chief? This was his idea!

SEVENTH CHIEF *(entering)*: Here I am. I had to find this long pole.

FIRST CHIEF: Your plan is not good! See, we are pushing and the sky is not moving.

SEVENTH CHIEF: Ah, but I said we must push together.

FIFTH CHIEF: We need a signal so that all can push together. Our people speak different languages.

SEVENTH CHIEF: Let us use YAH-HOO as the signal. Ready?

ALL: YES!

SEVENTH CHIEF: YAH-HOO.

(At the signal, everyone pushes together.)

ALL: YAH-HOO!

SEVENTH CHIEF: YAH-HOO.

(Again everyone pushes together.)

ALL: YAH-HOO!

TALL MAN: We are doing it!

MOTHER: Now my son won't be able to hide in the sky!

SEVENTH CHIEF: YAH-HOO.

(Again everyone pushes together.)

ALL: YAH-HOO!

BOY: It will be too high for my arrows to stick into it.

SEVENTH CHIEF: YAH-HOO.

(Again everyone pushes together.)

ALL: YAH-HOOOO!

FIRST CHIEF: We have done it!

NARRATOR: So the sky was pushed up. It was done by everyone working together. That night, though, when everyone looked overhead, they saw many stars in the sky. The stars were shining through the holes poked into the sky by the poles of everyone who pushed it up higher.

No one ever bumped his head on the sky again. And those stars are there to this day.

Think, Talk and Write

Talk About It Stage directors use sound effects and movements to help a play seem real for the audience. What sound effects and movements would you use in this play to help it seem real?

1. Use the pictures below to retell the play. **Retell**

2. How is *Pushing Up the Sky* similar to other stories you have read? **Compare and Contrast**

3. Pretend you are inviting a friend to see *Pushing Up the Sky* and she asks you what the play is about. How would you summarize it for her? **Summarize**

4. *Narrator* is a word that often appears in plays. What other words in the story are "play words"? **Vocabulary**

Look Back and Write Look back at the question on page 345. Think about the problems the characters describe at the beginning of the play. Now that you've read *Pushing Up the Sky*, write a response to the question.

Meet author **Joseph Bruchac on page 447.**

Retell

  G2R3.1 Compare and contrast plots, settings, and characters presented by different authors.

Writing

Prompt *Pushing up the Sky* is a play that explains something in nature. Think about someone you would like to invite to watch you perform in a play. Now write an invitation asking that person to come to your play.

Student Model

January 22, 2010

Barbara Johnson

123 Elm Street

Townville, CA 12345

Dear Aunt Barbara,

    My class is putting on a play called "The Spider and the Mouse". I play the Wise Owl. I hope you can come! We are all very excited about it!

    What: "The Spider and the Mouse"

    When: February 18th, 2010

    Time: 6:30pm

    Where: Davis Elementary School

        5678 Main Street

        Townville, CA

Love,

Jamie

Conventions of an invitation include date, salutation, closing, and signature.

Helping verbs are used to form the tense in other verbs.

Invitations give the exact time and place of the event.

Use the model to help you write your own invitation.

W2.3b Write personal and formal letters, thank-you notes, and invitations: Include the date, proper salutation, body, closing, and signature.

357

People and Nature

Strategy Talk

Summarizing as you read will help you to focus on the main events in the beginning, middle, and end of the story. Summarizing important parts of the plot will help you remember and understand what you read.

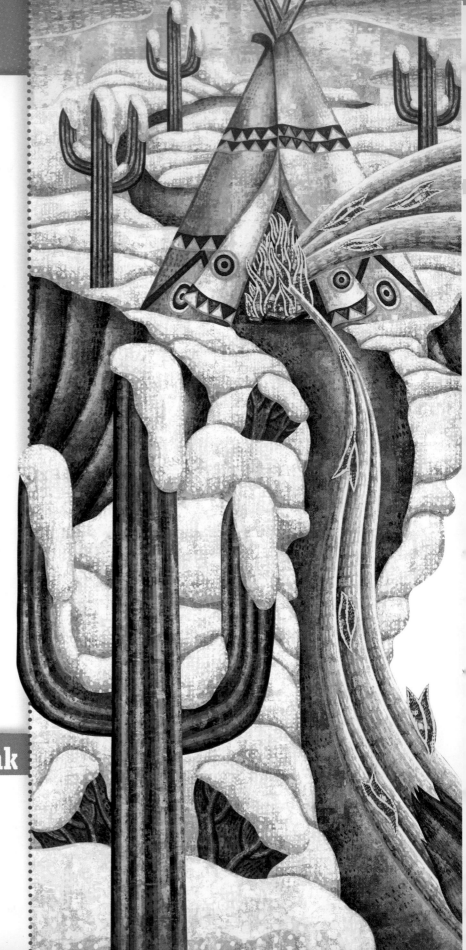

▶ **Ready to Try It?**
Read *Catch It and Run!* As you read, try to summarize the main events of the story to help you understand the plot.

Social Studies Link

Look in the library for other Native American myths about nature. Choose one to share with your class.

Catch It and *Run!*

from *When the World Was Young*
retold by Margaret Mayo
illustrated by Richard Downs

A long, long time ago, all fire belonged to three
Fire Beings who kept it hidden in their tepee, high on a
mountaintop. They would not share the fire with anyone
and guarded it carefully, night and day. So, when winter
came and the fierce winds howled and snow covered the
earth, men, women, and children had no way of warming
themselves. No fire. No hot food. Nothing at all.

Now Coyote, who is wise, knew about fire, and
one year, at winter's end, when he saw how cold and
miserable the people were, he decided to steal some
fire and give it to them. But how would he do it?

Coyote thought hard.

He called a meeting of the animals, and he said, "Who will help me steal some fire and give it to the people?" And Bear, Deer, Squirrel, Chipmunk, and Frog offered to help.

Coyote thought again.

"Bear," he said, "you are big and strong, so you must come with me to the Fire Beings' tepee. Deer, Squirrel, and Chipmunk, you are fast runners, so you must wait beside the trail, ready to run."

"What about me?" asked Frog. "I'd like to help!"

"Fro-og," sighed Coyote, shaking his head, "you're such a squatty little thing. You can jump and swim. But you can't run. There's nothing you can do."

"I could wait by the pond and be ready," said Frog. "Just in case. . . ."

"You do that," said Coyote. "Wait and be ready. Just in case. . . ."

That made Frog happy. He squatted down by the pond, and he waited while the others set off along the trail through the forest that led to the Fire Beings' mountaintop.

On the way Coyote stopped from time to time and told one of the animals to wait beside the trail. First Squirrel, next Chipmunk, and then Deer were left behind, and at last Bear and Coyote walked on alone.

When they reached the tepee on top of the mountain, Coyote told Bear to wait in the shadows until he heard Coyote call *"Aooo!"* Then Bear must make a big, loud rumpus.

Coyote crept up to the tepee. He gave a soft bark, and one of the Fire Beings opened the flap and looked out.

Coyote sort of trembled and said in his quietest, most polite voice, "My legs are freezing cold. May I please put them inside your warm tepee?"

He was so exceedingly polite that the Fire Being said, "Ye-es, all right. . . ."

Coyote stepped in his front legs, then he stepped in his back legs, and then he whisked in his tail. He looked longingly at the great blazing fire in the center of the tepee, but he said nothing. He just lay down and closed his eyes as if he were going to sleep. But the next moment he gave a long Coyote call, *"Aooo-ooo!"*

From outside the tepee came the sound of a big, loud rumpus as Bear growled and stamped about.

The Fire Beings all rushed out shouting, "Who's that?" And when they saw Bear, they chased him.

Coyote was ready. He grabbed a piece of burning wood between his teeth and away he ran, out of the tepee and down the mountain.

As soon as the Fire Beings saw Coyote with the firebrand, they abandoned Bear and chased Coyote.

Coyote ran and ran. He was fast, but the Fire Beings were faster, and they came closer.

Then Coyote saw Deer. "Catch it and *run!*" he called and threw the firebrand.

Deer caught it and ran. But he ran so fast that the wind fanned the fire out behind him, and a flame jumped onto his long tail and burned most of it. So that's why Deer has a shortish tail, even today.

Deer was fast, but the Fire Beings were faster, and they came closer.

Then Deer saw Chipmunk. "Catch it and *run!*" he called and threw the firebrand.

Chipmunk caught it and ran. But the Fire Beings came closer and closer, until one of them reached out an arm and clawed his back and left three long black stripes. And that's why Chipmunk has stripes on his back, even today.

Then Chipmunk saw Squirrel. "Catch it and *run!*" he called and threw the firebrand.

Squirrel caught it and ran. But the firebrand had been burning fast, and it was now so short that its great heat made Squirrel's bushy tail curl up over his back. And that's why Squirrel has a curled-up tail, even today.

Squirrel came to the pond. The Fire Beings were right at his back. What could he do?

Then he saw small, squatty Frog, waiting and ready. Just in case. . . .

"Catch it and *jump!*" called Squirrel and threw the firebrand, which was now quite tiny.

Frog caught the firebrand, but as he jumped one of the Fire Beings grabbed his tail and pulled it off. And that's why Frog has no tail, even today.

Now when Frog jumped, he landed in the pond, and to save the flames from the water, he gulped down the tiny firebrand. He held his breath and swam over to the other side of the pond.

Then Frog saw a tree. "Catch it and *hide!*" he called and coughed up all that was left of the firebrand, just a few bright flames.

And the tree caught the fire and hid it.

The Fire Beings ran around the pond, and they looked for the fire. But it was hidden in the tree, and they didn't know how to get it out again, so they returned to their home, high on the mountaintop.

But Coyote, who is wise, knew how to get fire out of the tree. He knew how to rub two dry sticks together to make a spark that could be fed with pine needles and pine cones and grow into a fire. It was Coyote who taught the people how to do this so that they need not be cold, ever again, in wintertime. And it was Coyote who went around and gave some fire to all the other trees, so that fire lies hidden in every tree, even today.

Reading Across Texts
What problems did you read about in *Pushing Up the Sky* and in *Catch It and Run!*? How are the problems alike? How are they different?

Writing Across Texts Make a chart that shows the problem and solution in each of these stories.

Let's Talk About
Investigating Nature

LS1.7 Use clear and specific vocabulary to communicate ideas and establish the tone.

Build Vocabulary

Learn ⊙ **Skill Unfamiliar Words** When you find an unfamiliar word in your reading, a dictionary or a glossary can help you find out its meaning. A dictionary gives the meaning of a word, and it also gives other information about words, such as part of speech, history, and pronunciation.

Practice Read "A Letter from Far Away" on page 369. List the highlighted words. Then use a dictionary or your glossary to find the meaning of each word. Write the meaning of each word.

Words to Know	temperature	shine	dim
	gigantic	gas	patterns
	ladle		

On Your Own Reread "A Letter from Far Away." Choose five words from the letter. Make a list of the words. Then look up each word in a dictionary. Write the part of speech for each word.

R1.7 Use a dictionary to learn the meaning and other features of unknown words.
R2.1 Use titles, tables of contents, chapter headings, glossaries, and indexes to locate information in text.

A Letter from Far Away

Dear Mom and Dad,

Grandpa and I are having a great time on our camping trip. We set up our tent right by the lake. I caught two fish today! The weather has been really hot. I hope the temperature goes down soon.

It's exciting to be so far away from the city. It is really dark here at night. I love the way the stars shine so brightly. These stars are nothing like the dim little dots we see in the city. Grandpa says that each star is a huge, gigantic ball of hot gas. That's amazing!

Grandpa and I like to look for patterns in the stars. Grandpa showed me some stars that form the shape of a ladle. I thought it looked more like a yo-yo than a big old spoon!

I'll mail this letter tomorrow, when we hike into town.

Love,
Darren

 **Need a Review?**
See *Words!*, p. W•14 for more information about using a glossary or dictionary.

 Ready to Try It?
Read *Seeing Stars*, pp. 372–383.

People and Nature

Build Comprehension

Learn ⊙ **Skill Draw Conclusions**

- A conclusion is a decision or opinion that makes sense based on facts and details.

- When you use information you read or already know to make decisions about a story, you are drawing conclusions.

- To check your conclusions, ask yourself, "Can I support my conclusion with facts from the story?" You may want to change your conclusion after you have finished the story.

Practice Read "Patterns in the Sky" on page 371. Look for facts and details that you can use to draw a conclusion.

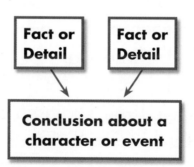

On Your Own **Write to Read** Reread "Patterns in the Sky." Use the graphic organizer above to help you draw a conclusion about why people named the constellations.

 Need a Review?
See *Picture It!*, p. PI•6 for more information about drawing conclusions.

▷ **Ready to Try It?**
As you read *Seeing Stars*, pp. 372–383, watch for and make your own conclusions.

  R2.4 Recall major points in the text and make and modify predictions about forthcoming information.

Patterns in the Sky

Long ago, people looked up at the night sky and noticed patterns in the stars. They gave these patterns names like *Libra, Draco,* and *Pisces.* Today we call these patterns *constellations.*

The Big Dipper is a star pattern that has inspired many stories. The seven stars of the Big Dipper are part of a constellation called *Ursa Major.* It is one of the most recognizable patterns in the sky. People have told stories about this group of stars for hundreds of years.

Many of the names of the constellations come from old stories. One constellation is called *Hercules.* This constellation is named after a brave hero from a Greek story. There are also constellations named after animals in old stories. One of these is *Leo,* named for a lion with skin so strong that no weapon could harm it.

One reason that constellations were given names was so that people would remember them. If people knew where a constellation was, they could figure out where Earth was in relation to the stars. This helped people long ago understand how the movement of the Earth was connected to seasons.

Skill You can use the details you've read so far to conclude that people have told stories about constellations for a long time.

Skill There are several facts in this paragraph. What conclusion can you make about why it was important to understand the constellations?

People and Nature

Seeing Stars

By Donna Latham

**How are stars different
from each other?**

It's a perfect night for stargazing. Twinkling stars, more than you can count, dot the dark sky. They glow like fireflies. Stars, pinpoints of light, line up in patterns, or constellations.

Why do stars only come out at night? Do the stars look the same? Which one moves—a star or the Earth? How can you connect stars to draw pictures in the sky? Find out, as you take a close-up look at these far-off fireballs!

How I Wonder *Where* You Are

Stars are always in the sky. During the day, you can't get a glimpse of them. Why? Sunlight fills the sky. Its brightness makes stars invisible. When the Earth changes position and the sun sets, it's starlight's turn to shine.

From Earth, stars look like specks of glitter. That's because they're so distant. Stars are actually gigantic spheres of fiery gas. Earth's star, the sun, is one of these fireballs. When you see it from Earth, the sun appears to be the largest star in the sky.

Yet, the sun is actually medium-sized. Why does it look so massive? In vast space, distances are enormous. Even at a whopping 93 million miles away, the sun is the star *closest* to Earth. Our brilliant neighbor looks much bigger than far-off stars.

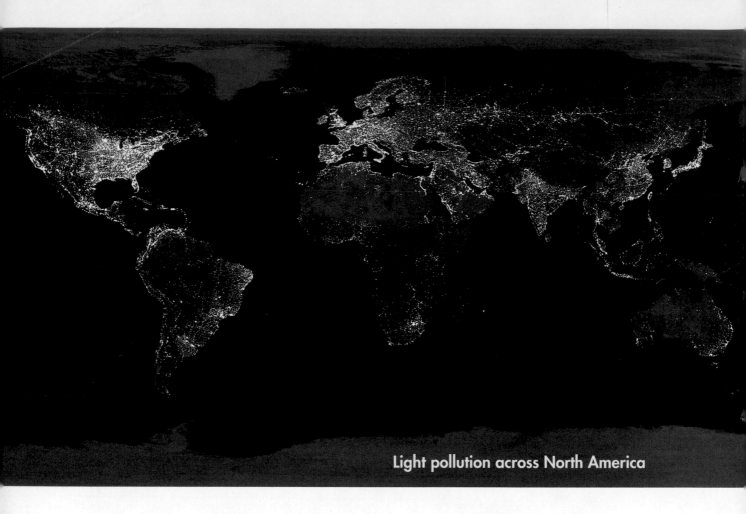

Light pollution across North America

Do you live in a city or large suburb? There, stars appear super-far away. Why? You're probably familiar with water, air, and noise pollution. Have you ever heard of light pollution? This intense nighttime light makes twinklers tough to see. In urban areas, smog can also block your view of stars.

When you are away from the city, you can see several thousand stars—with your eyes alone. They're part of our galaxy, the Milky Way. These stars give the impression they're close. In the country, it feels as if you can reach up and touch them.

See Far!

Other stars are so far-flung you can't see them without help. A telescope is just what the astronomer ordered! The word *telescope* is made of two Greek roots, *tele* and *scope*. *Tele* means "far." *Scope* means "see." A telescope makes distant objects appear much closer. That's not all . . . with a telescope, you can gaze at *millions* of stars.

When you peek up, you see that some stars shine brightly. Others are dim. At first, they all look white, but they're actually blue, white, yellow, and red. We think of the sun as very hot, but it's yellow, and blue stars have the hottest temperature. Red stars have the coolest.

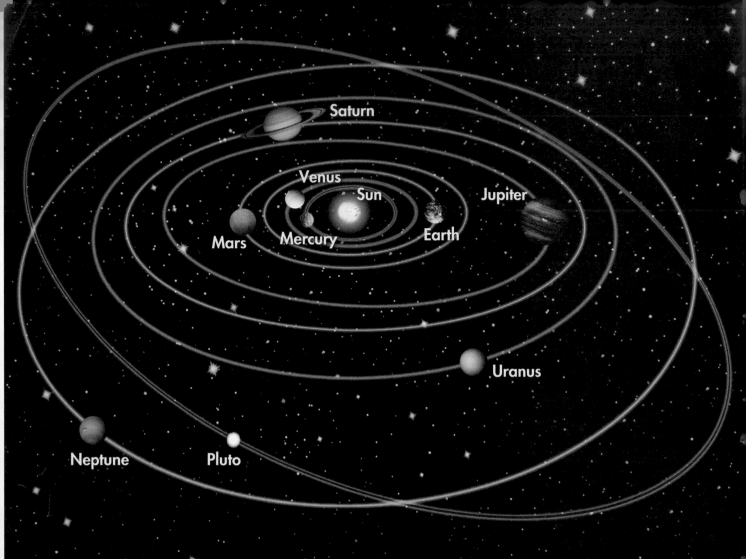

Moving Along

Have you ever noticed that stars appear to move?
You can track them with your eyes. Constellations drift
through the sky. From Earth, it looks like stars travel
around us. Yet, the opposite is true. The Earth moves.

You can't feel it, but right now you're riding a
huge merry-go-round. Earth spins through space as it
orbits the sun—and what goes around comes around!
Traveling at 1,000 miles per hour, it takes Earth
about 24 hours to spin completely. That makes the sky
change from day to night.

Connect the Stars

People have watched the stars for thousands of years. Stargazers in early times named constellations after animals, shapes, and characters from mythology. The stars have not changed locations since then. You can still gaze into the sky and connect stars to create the same shapes and patterns.

Constellation map

Hunt for Orion

People in different parts of the world can gaze at different constellations. Meet Orion, a gem of the Northern Hemisphere's winter sky, named after a boastful hunter from Greek mythology.

A sword swings from his belt, which is formed of three stars. He holds a starry shield. Orion has two of the sky's brightest stars. Betelgeuse, a gigantic red star, shines brilliantly at his shoulder. A scorching blue-white star called Rigel shines in Orion's left foot. Rigel is 50,000 times brighter than our sun!

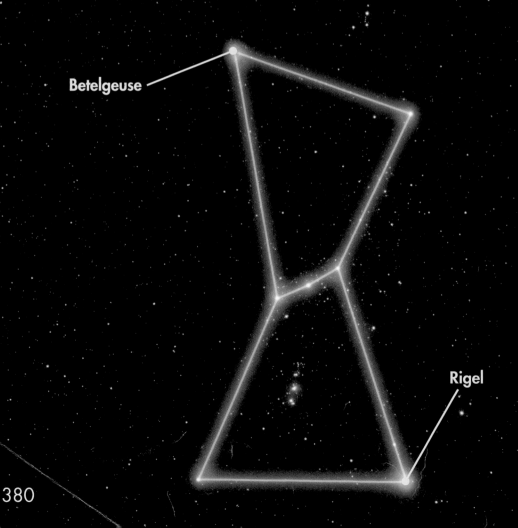

Betelgeuse

Rigel

Sirius, the Dog Star

Chase After Big Dog

Trotting after Orion is *Canis Major,* the Big Dog constellation. Big Dog has a head like a triangle and a perky tail. At its chest is blue-white Sirius, the Dog Star.

After the sun, Sirius is the brightest star we can see from Earth. That's because it's one of the stars closest to us even though it's nearly 6 trillion miles off! Its diameter is more than double the sun's.

In ancient times, people believed Sirius' bright light seared the Earth with summer heat. Today, the phrase "dog days of summer" describes the blistering period from July 3 to August 11. During this time, Sirius rises and sets with the sun.

Scoop Up the Big Dipper

The Big Dipper is a dazzler of the northern sky. It looks like a giant ladle. Connect the stars to see the Dipper's handle and bowl—but don't stop there! The Big Dipper is part of the *Ursa Major,* or Great Bear, constellation. The handle of the Dipper forms the bear's tail. The bowl is part of its body.

Because of Earth's movement, the Big Dipper's handle tips in different directions. The handle faces down in the winter. During the summer, it's up.

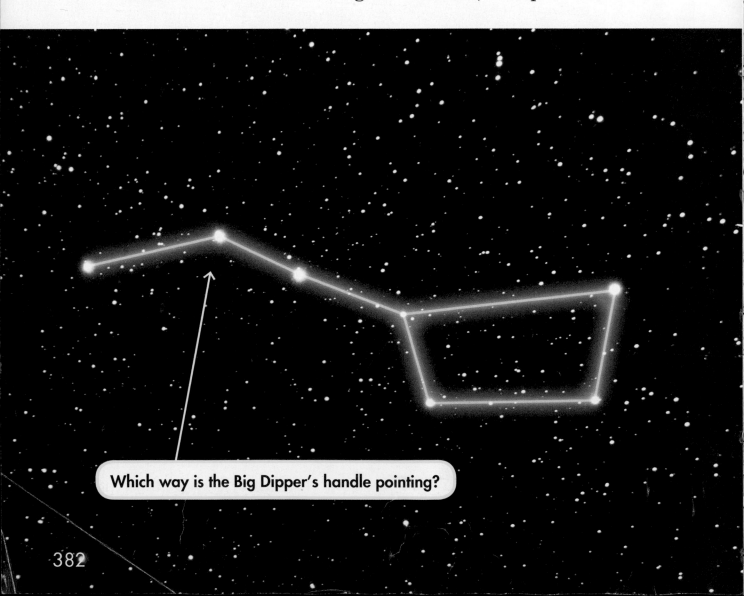

Which way is the Big Dipper's handle pointing?

So Vast It Needs a
New Word to Describe It!

Oh, my stars, the universe is ginormous! It appears to sprawl forever. How many stars does it hold altogether? No one knows for sure. NASA believes there are zillions. Astronomers claim that to tally all the stars would be as hard as counting grains of sand on a beach. It could take eons . . .

For now, keep seeing stars!

Think, Talk and Write

Talk About It Do you ever look at the stars? Tell a story about looking at stars.

1. Use the pictures below to summarize what you learned. **Summarize**

2. Did you use a graphic organizer to help you draw conclusions as you read? Talk about a conclusion you made and what facts helped you make it. **Draw Conclusions**

3. This selection gives a lot of information about stars. What questions did you ask while you were reading to better understand the information? **Ask Questions**

4. Did you find any unfamiliar words in your reading? Use a dictionary to learn the meaning of a new word from *Seeing Stars*. Then tell a friend what the word means. **Vocabulary**

Look Back and Write Look back at the question on page 373. What did you learn about stars that helps you answer the question? As you write your response, be sure to include details from the story to support your answer.

Meet author Donna Latham on page 448.

Summarize

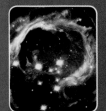     

R2.4 Recall major points in the text and make and modify predictions about forthcoming information.

Writing

Formal Letter

Prompt *Seeing Stars* explains what stars are. Think about something in nature you would like to investigate. Now write a formal letter to a scientist asking the questions that you would like to have answered.

Student Model

March 8, 2010

Professor M. Duncan

University of California

Los Angeles, CA 90095

Dear Professor Duncan,

   My name is Darnell Williams and I am interested in stars. My teacher helped me find your name on a list of college professors. She said you are a scientist who studies astronomy, so I am writing to ask you some questions.

   Which star is farthest away from Earth? Why do stars twinkle? How many stars are there? Do you have a telescope at home? I would also like to know how astronomy helps people.

   Thank you for reading my letter. I hope you will write me back.

   Sincerely,

   Darnell

A formal letter has a respectful tone.

Subjects and verbs must agree in number.

Letter focuses on one idea—asking questions about stars.

People and Nature

Use the model to help you write your own formal letter.

 W2.3b Write personal and formal letters, thank-you notes, and invitations: Include the date, proper salutation, body, closing, and signature.

385

Poetry Talk

Rhyme is the repetition of sounds in two or more words. These rhyming words are typically found at the ends of lines of poetry.

Ready to Try It?
As you read the poems from *Comets, Stars, the Moon, and Mars*, match the rhyming words together. Do you notice a pattern?

Science Link

Spend some time looking at the night sky. Start a journal of your observations. You could draw a picture of how the moon looks each night for a month. Or find a constellation chart at the library and use it to locate the North Star, the Big Dipper, and other stars and constellations.

386

Comets, Stars, the Moon, and Mars
by Douglas Florian

skywatch

On a clear night you might try
To gaze upon the starry sky.
A telescope or binoculars are
Great aids to observe a star.
To find your way it's good to sight
Upon a star that's very bright,
Like Sirius or Canopus,
Alpha Centauri or Arcturus.
You may see a planet or
A flash of light from a meteor.
Use a constellation chart
To help you tell the stars apart.
Start out when the day is done.
Most of all: Have lots of fun!

the solar system

Each planet orbits round the sun
(A somewhat circular path).
To calculate the time it takes
Requires lots of math.

Astronomers know the planets well,
Each mountain, ring, and moon.
But none has ever gone to one,
Nor will go to one soon.

the moon

A NEW moon isn't really new,
It's merely somewhat dark to view.

A CRESCENT moon may seem to smile,
Gladly back after a while.

A HALF moon is half dark, half light.
At Sunset look due south to sight.

A FULL moon is a sight to see,
Circular in geometry.

After full, the moon will wane
Night by night, then start again.

Reading Across Texts
Seeing Stars was written to give readers information.
Why do you think Mr. Florian wrote these poems?

Writing Across Texts Use what you have learned
to write your own poem about stars.

Let's Talk About

Helping Animals

LS1.7 Use clear and specific vocabulary to communicate ideas and establish the tone.

People and Nature

Build Vocabulary

Learn ⊙ **Skill Suffixes** Remember, suffixes are word parts added to the end of a word to change the meaning. Adding suffixes to words can change their parts of speech. The suffix *-ly* added to a word means "in a ____way." It can change an adjective to an adverb, or a word that describes a verb.

Practice Read "Breaking the Ice" on page 391. Make a list of all the words that have suffixes. Use the meaning of the suffix to figure out what each word means.

Words to Know	surrounded	channel	bay
	blizzards	supplies	anxiously
	chipped	melody	symphony

On Your Own Reread "Breaking the Ice." Write all the adverbs you can find in the passage. Then circle the adverbs that have the suffix *-ly*. Beside the circled adverbs, write the word without the suffix. Use the adverbs in a sentence.

R1.8 Use knowledge of prefixes (e.g., *un-, re-, pre-, bi-, mis-, dis-*) and suffixes (e.g., *-er, -est, -ful*) to determine the meaning of words.

Breaking the Ice

Josh is a sailor on a Canadian icebreaker. An icebreaker is a ship with a heavy steel bow, or front, that it uses to break through ice. Sometimes a ship, surrounded on all sides by ice, becomes trapped and can't move. The icebreaker carefully cuts a channel through the ice so that the ship can easily sail to safety.

Josh likes helping people. One winter, a waterfront village on a bay in the far north had been buried by blizzards. The people were quickly running out of food and other supplies. No one could get to the village over land, so the villagers called the icebreaker for help.

The ship had to cut a path through the ice on the bay. The people were nervous and watched the ship anxiously. They chipped away the ice around the dock so that the ship could get close enough to safely unload the supplies. As the ship sailed away, the villagers began to sing a song. Josh did not know the melody, or tune, but he truly enjoyed the symphony of voices saying *thank you*.

 Need a Review?
See *Words!*, p. W•6 for more information about suffixes.

 Ready to Try It?
Read *A Symphony of Whales*, pp. 394–409.

People and Nature

Build Comprehension

⊙ **Skill** **Generalize**

- As you read, you will sometimes find several facts or ideas that go together. When you make a statement that puts the ideas together, you generalize.

- Sometimes the author makes generalizations for you, and sometimes you have to make them for yourself.

- Clue words such as *most, many, all,* or *few* can help you recognize generalizations authors make.

Practice Read "Songbirds of the Sea" on page 393 to find generalizations the author has made for you.

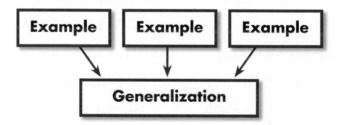

On Your Own **Write to Read** Reread "Songbirds of the Sea" and make a generalization of your own. Or make a generalization about things you see in your classroom. Use the graphic organizer above to show the relationships in your own generalization.

 Need a Review?
See *Picture It!,* p. PI•8 for additional help with generalizations.

 Ready to Try It?
As you read *A Symphony of Whales,* pp. 394–409, watch for and make your own generalizations.

🐻 **G5R2.4** Draw inferences, conclusions, or generalizations about text and support them with textual evidence and prior knowledge.

Songbirds of the Sea

Beluga whales make lots of noise. They click, whistle, squeal, and grunt. They also sing. Because belugas sing so much, they are called songbirds of the sea.

Why do belugas make so much noise? Sometimes they want to talk to each other. At other times, they make noise to find things. That often means food. They may be trying to attract a mate. Beluga whales make noise for many important reasons.

Usually light from the sun does not reach ocean waters below about 325 feet. A beluga whale generally swims deeper than that. Since the whale can't see, it makes sounds. The sounds bounce off an object and back to the whale. This tells the whale where the object is. If it is a fish, the whale has found dinner.

All belugas use sound to move through ocean waters. Sound waves help a whale know where the ocean bottom is, as well as where objects are, such as rocks, boats, and icebergs.

Skill Here the author makes a generalization about the sounds beluga whales make.

Skill After reading these two facts, you can make a generalization about where beluga whales swim.

People and Nature

A Symphony of
Whales

by Steve Schuch
illustrated by Wendell Minor

Can people communicate
with whales?

From the earliest time she could remember, Glashka had heard music inside her head. During the long, dark winters, blizzards sometimes lasted for days. Then her family stayed indoors, close to the small fire. Glashka heard the songs calling to her out of the darkness, beyond even the voice of the wind.

The old ones of her village said, "That is the voice of Narna, the whale. Long has she been a friend to our people. She was a friend of our grandparents' grandparents; she was a friend before we saw the boats of strange men from other lands. But it is long now

since one of us has heard her. It is a great gift you have."
And Glashka would fall asleep, wrapped in her sealskin
blanket, remembering their words.

The sea gave life to Glashka's village. The seals gave
meat and warm furs to protect against the winter cold. In
summer the people caught salmon and other fish, then
salted them to keep for the hard times to come. And from
Narna, the whale, the people received food for themselves
and their sled dogs, waterproof skins for their parkas and
boots, and oil for their lamps in the long winter darkness.

One year the snows came early. For three days a
blizzard bore down on the village. When it finally stopped,
Glashka's family needed supplies from the next village.
Glashka asked if she might help drive the sled dogs. "It is
not so easy to drive the sled," her parents said. "The dogs
will know if you are uncertain of the way. But you will
know the way home. Perhaps on the way back, you may
try. Now go to sleep."

That night in her dreams, Glashka drove the dogsled.
But the dogs did not follow her commands. Instead they
led her to open water surrounded by ice. Glashka heard
the singing of Narna, louder than she had ever heard
it before. She awoke in the darkness of her sealskins,
wondering what the dream had meant.

The morning was clear and cold as the family set out.
The dogs made good time to the neighboring village.
Before starting back, Glashka's parents packed the
supplies into the sled. Glashka checked the dogs' feet for
cuts. She rubbed their ears and necks. Glashka's parents
gave her the reins. "We'll follow behind you. If your heart

and words are clear, the dogs will listen and take you where you wish to go."

They set off. Across the ice, snow swirled as the wind began to pick up. Suddenly the sled dogs broke from the trail, yelping and twitching their ears. "What is it?" Glashka's parents shouted.

"I think they hear something," Glashka called back.

The sled dogs pulled harder. Their keen ears could pick up high-pitched notes that most humans couldn't hear. But Glashka, if she turned just right, could make out the eerie moans and whistles that grew louder until even her parents could hear them.

The dogs stopped short. They were right at the edge of a great bay of open water, surrounded on all sides by ice and snow.

Everywhere Glashka looked, the water seemed to be heaving and boiling, choked with white whales. Her father came up beside her. "Beluga whales," he said softly.

Glashka stared. "There must be more than a thousand of them."

The cries of the whales rose and fell on the wind as they swam slowly about. The dogs whined and pawed anxiously at the ice. "Let's hurry to the village," cried Glashka. "We'll get help!"

399

Glashka's father, though, knew there was no help. "They must have been trapped when they came here last fall looking for food," he said quietly. "There's nothing we can do to free them. When the last of the water freezes over, the whales will die."

But Glashka's mother remembered that an icebreaker, several winters ago, had rescued a Russian freighter trapped in the sea ice. "Could we call on the emergency radio? Maybe an icebreaker can clear a channel for the whales," she said.

Glashka and her parents raced back to their village. They gathered everyone together and told them what had happened. Glashka's father got on the emergency radio and put out a distress call. "Beluga whales, maybe thousands of them, trapped. We need an icebreaker. Can anyone hear me?"

Far out at sea, a great Russian icebreaker named the *Moskva* picked up the faint signal. "We read you," the captain radioed back. "We're on our way, but it may take us several weeks to reach you. Can you keep the whales alive until then?"

Some of the people from Glashka's village started setting up a base camp near the whales. Others set out by dogsled to alert the surrounding settlements.

Everyone came—young and old, parents, grandparents, and children. Day after day they chipped back the edges of the ice, trying to make more room for the whales to come up to breathe. "Look," said Glashka's grandmother. "See how the whales are taking turns, how they give the younger ones extra time for air."

As Glashka took her turn chipping back the ice, the song of Narna filled her ears again. She sang to the whales while she worked, trying to let them know help was on the way. Each day, Glashka looked anxiously for a ship. But each day, a little more water turned to ice. Each day, the whales got weaker from hunger.

Glashka knew how it felt to be hungry. The year before, her village had caught barely enough fish to make it through to spring. Sometimes the memory still gnawed at her. Even so, she gave the whales part of the fish from her lunch. The other villagers noticed and began to feed some of their own winter fish to the whales too.

One morning Glashka awoke to the sounds of excited voices and barking dogs. The icebreaker had broken through the main channel during the night. "Hurry,

Glashka," her parents called. Glashka pulled on her boots and parka and ran down the path to the water.

Everyone was gathered. Off to one side, the old ones stood, watching. They beckoned Glashka to join them. "Now," they said, "let us see what the whales will do."

The whales crowded together in fear, keeping as far from the icebreaker as possible. On board the ship, the captain gave orders. He hoped the whales would see the pathway cleared through the ice and follow the ship to safety. The icebreaker slowly turned around and faced back out to sea.

But the whales wouldn't follow the ship. "They may be afraid of the noise of our engines," the captain radioed to shore. "I've heard that trapped whales will sometimes follow the singing of other whales. We'll try playing a recording of whale songs."

Glashka felt a shiver down her back. "Narna's songs," she whispered to the sled dogs. "They're going to play Narna's songs."

Then the songs of the whales echoed over the water—deep moans and high whistling calls, ancient sounds from another world.

But the whales would not go near the ship. Again and again, the captain inched the giant icebreaker closer to the whales, then back toward the sea. But the whales stayed as far away as they could.

"It's no use," the captain radioed in despair. "And we can't stay beyond tomorrow. Already the channel is starting to refreeze!"

Glashka was near tears as she asked the old ones what could be done now. "Wait," they said. "Let us see what tomorrow brings."

That night the song of Narna came to Glashka again. Only this time it was different. She heard the music and voices of whales, but she heard other music too . . . melodies she'd never before. . . . While it was still dark, Glashka woke her parents. "I've heard Narna again," she said. "And I've heard other music too!"

"You have to tell the old ones," Glashka's parents said.

The old ones of the village listened carefully as Glashka told them what she had heard. "So, it is other music Narna is asking for," they said thoughtfully. "Long is the time, but once, it is said, humans and whales made music together. Perhaps the time has come again. Let us speak with the captain!"

Quickly Glashka and the old ones radioed the ship. "Have you any other music, people music, to play for the whales?" they asked. The captain said he would see what his crew could find.

First, they tried playing rock and roll. The electric guitars and drums boomed, but the whales would not follow the ship.

Next, the crew tried Russian folk music. It was softer, with many voices singing together. The whales swam a little closer, but still they would not follow the ship.

On shore, Glashka ran back to the radio transmitter. She had to talk with the captain. "I *know* there's other music that will work. Please keep trying!" she told him.

The crew found some classical music. First the sweet sounds of violins and violas, next the deeper notes of the cellos and, deepest of all, the string basses . . . and way up high, a solo violin. . . .

Everyone fell silent as the melody carried over the water. The whales grew quiet, too, listening.

A few whales started to sing back to the ship and to each other. Gradually more whales joined in.

Then . . . they began to swim toward the ship!

Cautiously the captain started the huge engines and headed slowly out to sea. One whale followed, then another, then a few more. Soon all the whales were following the ship through the narrow channel, past the broken chunks of ice, back to the safety of the open ocean.

On shore, people laughed and cried and hugged each other. The sled dogs jumped up and barked, trying to lick the noses and faces of anyone they could reach. Glashka buried her wet face in the fur of the dogs' necks. "Such good, good dogs," she told them over and over. "Such good dogs. Now the whales are going home!"

On board the ship, the captain and his crew raised every flag. The music played as the captain radioed to say the whales were safe. He and his crew were finally going home too.

Glashka and her family looked out to sea. They waved to the icebreaker and the disappearing whales. "And do you hear Narna singing now?" her grandmother asked.

"Yes," Glashka said, "but it isn't just Narna I hear now. It's something bigger than that . . . something like a whole symphony of whales!"

Think, Talk and Write

Talk About It What do you think was the most exciting part of the story? Why was that part exciting?

1. Use the pictures below to retell the story. **Retell**

2. Think about the lives of the villagers and the lives of the whales. Do their lives show how people and nature are connected? **Generalize**

3. At the end of the story, Glashka tells the sled dogs that they are good dogs. Why does she believe they are good dogs? **Answer Questions**

4. The words *symphony* and *melody* are related to music. What other words from the story could you include in that group? **Vocabulary**

TEST PRACTICE

Look Back and Write Look back at the question on page 395. Now that you've read *A Symphony of Whales*, do you think people can communicate with whales? What did you find in the story to support your answer? Write a paragraph explaining your thoughts. Be sure to include details from the story.

Meet author **Steve Schuch on page 450** and illustrator **Wendell Minor on page 449.**

Retell

R2.2 Ask questions and support answers by connecting prior knowledge with literal information found in, and inferred from, the text.

Writing

Prompt A *Symphony of Whales* is a narrative that tells the realistic story of a girl who helps whales. Think about ways in which people help animals. Now write a realistic story about someone who helps an animal.

Writing Trait

Connect short, choppy **sentences** to make your writing flow.

Student Model

Ling's Kitten

Ling is excited because today she is going to adopt a kitten. She has wanted a kitten for a long time.

Ling and her father go to the animal shelter. Ling sees cages full of dogs and cats waiting for homes. In the last cage she sees a kitten that looks sad and lonely. Ling takes the kitten home.

Ling names the kitten Henry and gives him lots of love. Soon Henry is happy.

Story has made-up characters and a setting that seem real.

Present tense verbs show action taking place now.

Connecting word joins short sentences.

Use the model to help you write your own realistic story.

W2.1b Write narratives: Include well-chosen details to develop the plot.

411

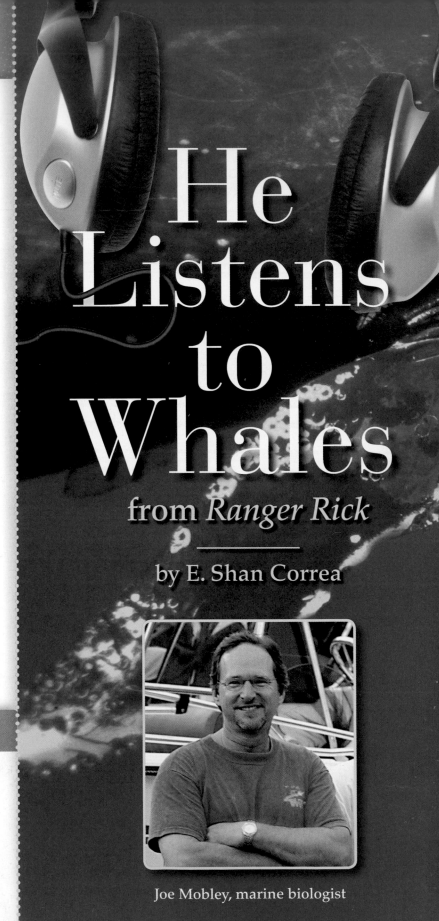

He Listens to Whales

from *Ranger Rick*

by E. Shan Correa

Joe Mobley, marine biologist

> *Humpback whales chatter and call to each other—and they sing songs for hours. What does all this humpback "hollering" mean? Here's one scientist who's trying to find out.*

Joe Mobley lives near the island of Maui in Hawaii. (*Maui* rhymes with *"zowie."*) It's the perfect place for a scientist who studies how humpback whales behave. The whales hang out near Maui all winter long.

Joe has lots of questions about these huge mammals. How do they know where to go when they travel through the ocean? How do they find each other? How do groups stay together? Joe thinks clues to these mysteries are held in the sounds that these whales make. To collect clues, he listens to the humpbacks.

Whale Chatter

"Humpbacks make three main types of sounds," Joe explains. "Both the males and the females call loudly when they're hungry or eating. Males 'talk' when they're hanging out in groups. And males sing during mating time."

Joe first heard the whales' feeding calls from a tape that another scientist had made. The whales were feeding in their summer home off the coast of Alaska. All were scooping up small fish and shrimp-like krill with their enormous mouths. And they seemed to call to each other while they ate. "You can imagine how noisy they were!" Joe says with a laugh. "They eat all the time during the summer," he continues, "but they almost never eat during the winter."

To listen to whales in winter, Joe doesn't have to go far. He just heads to their winter home in the ocean around Maui. That's when he hears the second kind of whale sound, which he calls "talking."

Joe explains what the sounds may mean: "Whales hang out in groups called *pods*. While they're in pods, the male whales make strange clicks, creaks, roars, and whines. Some of them seem to be signaling to females, as if they were saying, 'Hey, I'm over here!' Or they might be saying to other males, 'This is my mate, so stay away.' So far, no one has heard females or young whales 'talking' in this way."

This scientist is listening for whale calls.

These scientists are recording humpback whale songs.

Long Songs

Whale songs are the third kind of sound that Joe studies. You may have heard them on records. Some parts of a whale's song sound sad, like children crying. Some parts are high squeaks. And some rumble like thunder.

"These songs are beautiful, but *loud!*" Joe says. "They're much louder than any other animal sound, louder even than rock music. Our boat shakes when a singing whale is close by."

A humpback's song has parts that are repeated over and over. One song can last 30 minutes.

Then the whale might repeat the whole song. Sometimes a humpback sings for more than 20 hours without stopping!

Reading Across Texts
You have read *A Symphony of Whales* about beluga whales and "He Listens to Whales" about humpback whales. What do the two kinds of whales have in common?

Writing Across Texts Create a Venn diagram to compare and contrast the two kinds of whales.

Let's Talk About
Impacting
Nature

Build Vocabulary

Learn ⊙ **Skill Prefixes** are word parts added to the beginning of a word to change the meaning. You can use what you know about prefixes to understand the meaning of a word you do not know. For example, the prefix *re-* means "again," so *retell* means "to tell again."

Practice Read "Is This Water Safe to Drink?" on page 419. Think about the words with prefixes. Find two that start with the prefix *un-*. Look them up in a dictionary and try to find out what the prefix means.

Words to Know	refreshing	digest	liquid
	conserve	impurities	dissolved
	substances	condenses	

On Your Own Reread "Is This Water Safe to Drink?" Find a word that begins with the prefix *re-*. Think of as many words as you can that start with *re-*. Write them down and then their meanings.

R1.7 Use a dictionary to learn the meaning and other features of unknown words.
R1.8 Use knowledge of prefixes (e.g., *un-, re-, pre-, bi-, mis-, dis-*) and suffixes (e.g., *-er, -est, -ful*) to determine the meaning of words.

Is This Water Safe to Drink?

Some people like to visit nature. They may camp in a forest or sail on a quiet sea.

But what do people do if they want to visit a place and discover they are unable to drink the water? People need refreshing water to cool off, digest food, and keep their bodies working well.

Sometimes people who are camping or sailing bring their own water with them. But a liquid like water can be very heavy. They usually can't bring a lot. This means they must conserve and not misuse their water.

People who are camping or sailing may want to drink water found in a lake or in the ocean. This water may look safe to drink, but it is probably unclean. Impurities, such as germs, may have dissolved in the water. It might also contain substances like salt that are not good to drink.

There are ways to clean the water so you can reuse it. One way to kill germs is to boil water for at least one minute. There are also ways to remove salt from seawater. People can heat the water and collect the clean water that condenses inside a container.

Need a Review?
See *Words!*, p. W•5 for more information about prefixes.

Ready to Try It?
Read *Did a Dinosaur Drink This Water?*, pp. 422–435.

People and Nature

Build Comprehension

Learn ◉ **Skill Draw Conclusions**

- A conclusion is a decision you reach after thinking about the facts and details you read.

- As you read, think about the details, facts, and what you already know to help draw conclusions about character and plot.

- After reading ask yourself, "Does my conclusion make sense?"

Practice Read "Where Does the Water Go?" on page 421. Look for facts and details that you can use to draw a conclusion.

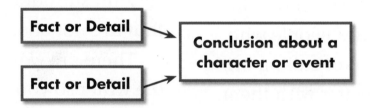

On Your Own **Write to Read** Reread "Where Does the Water Go?" Think about the conclusion the author makes about saving water. Write a short paragraph about another way people can conserve water.

- - - - - - - - - -

 Need a Review?
See *Picture It!*, p. PI·6 for more information about drawing conclusions.

 Ready to Try It?
As you read *Did a Dinosaur Drink This Water?*, pp. 422–435, watch for facts and details that help you draw conclusions.

R2.2 Ask questions and support answers by connecting prior knowledge with literal information found in, and inferred from, the text.

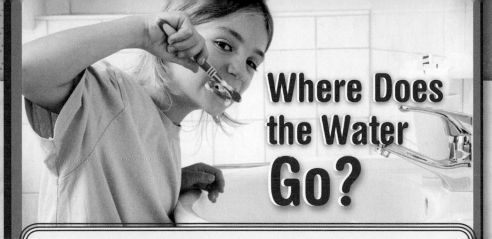

Where Does the Water Go?

Water is a big part of our lives. We can't live without it! People should always be careful not to waste water. This is true for everyone, not just those who live in dry places. There are many things people can do to help conserve, or save, water.

One easy thing everyone can do is to try to use less water when brushing teeth. This means turning off the water while you are brushing. When you are ready to rinse, turn the water back on. Also, people should make sure their faucets do not drip. Over time, a dripping faucet can waste enough water to fill a large pool!

If you have a dishwasher in your home, don't run it until it is full. Running a dishwasher with just a few dishes is a big waste of water.

Think about all the different ways you use water in your home. With just a few changes, you may be able to save a lot of water every year.

Skill Put these facts together with what you already know about the many uses of water. Can you draw a conclusion about why it is important to conserve water?

Skill Here is another chance to draw a conclusion. Think about why running a half-empty dishwasher is wasteful.

People and Nature

Genre **Expository nonfiction** gives facts about the real world. Look for facts about water.

Did a Dinosaur Drink This Water?

Author: Robert E. Wells

Illustrator: Nancy Woodman

How could a dinosaur drink the same water as you?

Every living thing needs water. Without it, flowers and apple trees will never grow. Fish live in water, ducks swim on top of water, and people need to drink it every day.

Water dissolves minerals and food substances, or NUTRIENTS, and carries them inside living things. When you water an apple tree, the water dissolves minerals in the soil. The water-mineral mix is absorbed by the roots and drawn up through the tree trunk to the leaves. Then the leaves, using water, air and the sun's energy produce nutrients for the apples.

When you eat an apple, the nutrients are digested in your body— which is made mostly of water. Then your blood, which is also mostly water, carries the nutrients to every part of your body— giving you energy for everything you do!

Water comes in 3 forms: LIQUID, SOLID, and GAS. When it's liquid, it pours. When it's solid, it's ice. When it's heated, it EVAPORATES, changing into WATER VAPOR, an invisible gas.

On a warm day, there's nothing more refreshing than a cold glass of ice-cold water. But the water we drink every day isn't new. It's been recycled—not just once, but thousands of times! It's because water is constantly renewed and cleaned by a big recycling system—Earth's WATER CYCLE.

If you pour a glass of water into a stream, it mixes with the stream and keeps on flowing. As the stream flows down the mountain, some of the impurities that are always in stream water are filtered out as the water passes over and through rocks, pebbles, and plants.

Flowing streams are one of nature's ways of cleaning water as it moves through the water cycle.

If you keep following the stream you'll discover it flows into a river and mixes with the river water.

Often, small rivers flow into bigger rivers. Sooner or later, the bigger rivers flow into the ocean. Ocean water and river water are not the same. River water is FRESH WATER, and ocean water has lots of salt.

Even so, the waters mix and the river water becomes part of the ocean. But that is not the end of the story. Water doesn't stay in the ocean.

The sun heats the water on the surface of the ocean, and the water turns into its gas form: water vapor. Aided by the wind, the water vapor rises in the air. When it meets colder air, the vapor CONDENSES, or goes back to its liquid form.

It changes into billions of tiny water droplets we see as clouds. The water in clouds is fresh, because as ocean water evaporates, it leaves the salt and other impurities behind. Evaporation is one of nature's best water cleaners.

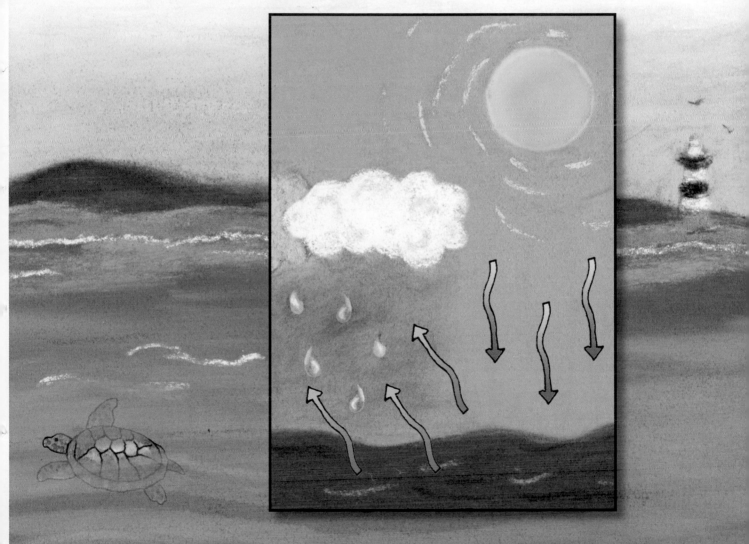

Now the wind blows some of the clouds over land, and when the water droplets build up and grow heavier they fall as rain—or snow, if the air is cold.

Some of the rain and snow falls right back into streams, rivers, and the ocean—but not *all* of it. At least, not for a while.

Some of the water seeps underground, and stays near the surface. Some water may sink deeper into the ground and collect in rocky areas called AQUIFIERS.

Water may remain stored underground for hundreds of years.

Some snow falls on high mountains, where it's always below freezing. As the snow builds up, its great weight compresses it into solid ice, forming GLACIERS.

Some snow falls near the North and South Poles, where it is very cold, and becomes part of the polar ice. ICEBERGS are chunks of polar ice floating in the ocean.

Water may stay frozen in glaciers and polar ice for thousands of years. Most of Earth's fresh water is frozen in polar ice and glaciers—or stored under ground!

Eventually, most of the underground water seeps out into rivers, lakes, and the ocean. Polar ice and glaciers melt and become part of ocean water.

Ocean water evaporates, and the cycle repeats—over and over and over again.

Earth's oceans are huge. They cover about 70% of Earth's surface and contain about 97% of Earth's water.

All water evaporates, but the oceans are so big, they play the biggest part in Earth's water cycle. The ocean is also a home, or HABITAT, for sea plants, fish, and creatures like crabs and octopuses. All these need salt water to live. Millions of people depend on fish and other sea life for food every day.

Streams, rivers and lakes are fresh water. They provide habitats for living things that need fresh water—plants and trees, birds, insects, and animals.

The fresh water in lakes and rivers is used by people for drinking, washing, cooking, and growing food. We sail on it, swim in, and fish in it. Lake and river water can even make the lights in your house go on!

Some rivers have DAMS. A dam is a huge wall that controls the flow of the river. The water that is held back collects in a lake, or RESERVOIR, behind the dam. When the reservoir water is released and flows through the dam, it creates energy to make electricity.

Electricity made with flowing water is called HYDROELECTRICITY.

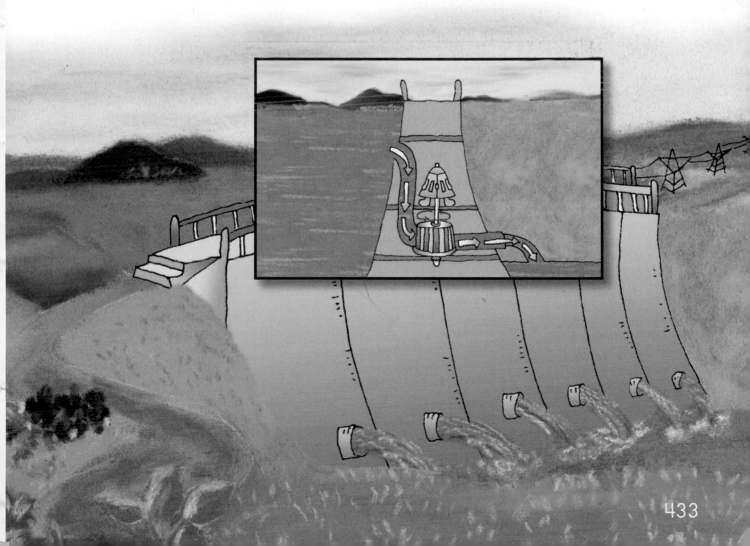

Reservoir water flows through big pipes inside the dam. The tremendous force of the flowing water spins the blades on water turbines, which are connected to generators. Then the water flows back into the river.

Usually, a dam has many generators. Together, they supply electricity to nearby farms, towns, and cities.

We cannot survive on Earth without water—so we must all take care of it! Yet WATER POLLUTION is a problem all over the world. Toxic chemicals from landfills an factories can poison water. Garbage and sewage in water can cause germs to spread, making people, animals, and fish sick.

Scientists say there is enough fresh water in the world for everyone—if we practice CONSERVATION, protecting water and using only what we need.

Water belongs to everyone, so helping take care of it is everyone's job. If we all help conserve and protect water—even helping in a small way—there will always be delicious water to drink—even if a dinosaur drank it first!

Think, Talk and Write

Talk About It Have you ever wondered, "How could our planet run without water?" Talk about how this story helped you understand why we need to protect and conserve water.

1. Use the pictures below to summarize what you learned. **Summarize**

2. What conclusions were you able to make during your reading? Tell a friend about one of your conclusions. **Draw Conclusions**

3. This selection talks about some really big ideas. Which parts might you want to reread or review to make sure you understand? **Monitor and Clarify**

4. Two of the Words to Know on p. 418 begin with the prefix *con-*. What other words with prefixes did you see in your reading? **Vocabulary**

Look Back and Write Look back at the question on page 423. Think about what you learned about the water cycle. Now write a short paragraph explaining whether a dinosaur could drink the same water as you. Be sure to include story details to support your answer.

Summarize

R2.4 Recall major points in the text and make and modify predictions about forthcoming information.

Writing

Formal Letter

Prompt *Did a Dinosaur Drink This Water?* explains the role of water in nature. Think about how you impact nature around you. Now write a letter to a science magazine, asking how you could impact nature in a more positive way.

Student Model

April 21, 2010

ASK Magazine

30 Grove Street, Suite C

Peterborough, NH 03458

Dear ASK Editor,

I am a third grader at Washington Elementary School in California. My class is studying recycling. We read an article from your magazine about how to reduce waste by reusing things.

I would like to know other ways in which kids like me can help protect nature. My older brother told about something called sustainable living. He says it means protecting the environment. Could you please print an article that explains what it is?

Your articles for kids who care about the environment are very helpful and educational. Thank you for making such a great magazine.

Sincerely,

Sara

A formal letter is short and to the point.

Irregular verbs do not follow typical spelling patterns.

An inter-rogative sentence ends with a question mark.

Use the model to help you write your own formal letter.

 W2.3.a Write personal and formal letters, thank-you notes, and invitations: Show awareness of the knowledge and interests of the audience and establish a purpose and context.

437

People and Nautre

Search Engines help you find Web sites on the Internet. Use keywords to find a Web site on your topic. The search engine window is where you type in a keyword. Click on the SEARCH button to see the results. Each item on the list is a link to a Web site that contains your keyword.

 Ready to Try It?
As you read "The Water Cycle," use the text boxes to help you understand how an Internet search works.

Science Link

Try your own Internet search. Use the phrase "water cycle experiment" as your keywords/search term. Look for an experiment or demonstration of the water cycle that you could safely share with your class.

The Water Cycle

You just learned how water is recycled again and again. If you want to learn more about how the water cycle works, you could try searching the Internet.

for more practice

Get Online!

PearsonSuccessNet.com

You type the keywords *"water cycle"* into a search engine and click SEARCH. If you search using a phrase, it helps to put the phrase in quotation marks.

File

Search Engine | "water cycle" | search

The search engine you choose might offer a list of Web sites about the water cycle. You might find results such as the following.

File   Edit

1. The **Water Cycle**. A Bibliography. This bibliography lists books about the water cycle.

2. A diagram demonstrating the **Water Cycle**. This diagram shows how water enters the atmosphere through evaporation and comes back to the earth through condensation.

3. The **Water Cycle** is a constant action in nature. You can see the water cycle at work by doing this experiment at home.

The second link to the Water Cycle may seem interesting to you. You click on it.

When you click on the link, you might see a computer screen such as this:

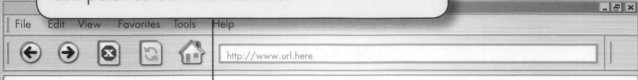

File   Edit   View   Favorites   Tools   Help

http://www.url.here

The Water Cycle

The water cycle is a continuous action happening in nature. Whether you realize it or not, all water is part of the water cycle. The water that comes out of your faucet has just an important role in the water cycle as the ocean does.

- Bodies of Water
- Diagrams
- Experiments
- Recycling Water
- **Steps in the Water Cycle**
- Weather

If you click on Steps in the Water Cycle, this is what you might find.

File   Edit   View   Favorite

Steps in the Water Cycle

The water cycle consists of 3 main steps. Water found on land or in water warms up and turns to water vapor through evaporation. Water vapor cools and condenses. When it condenses, it turns into precipitation. The water returns to land as rain, snow, sleet, or fog. The water on land returns to a river or lake, and finally the ocean where the water cycle begins again.

If you click on Diagrams, this is what you might find.

File   Edit   View   Favorites   Tools   Help

http://www.url.here

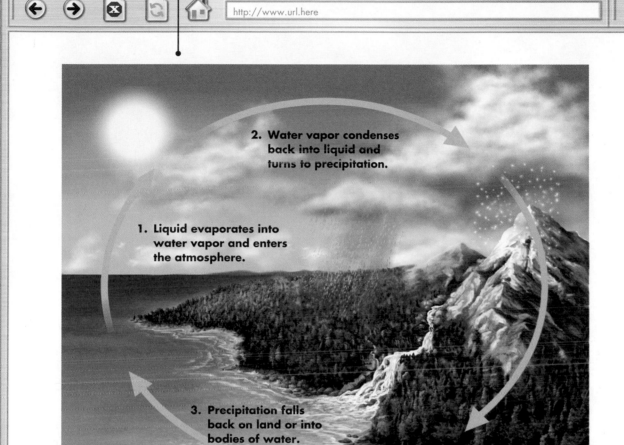

2. Water vapor condenses back into liquid and turns to precipitation.

1. Liquid evaporates into water vapor and enters the atmosphere.

3. Precipitation falls back on land or into bodies of water.

Reading Across Texts

Did a Dinosaur Drink This Water? includes information about the water cycle and "The Water Cycle" explains how to use the Internet to find out more about this topic. Make a list of keywords you could use in another Internet search about water.

Writing Across Texts Draw your own diagram of the water cycle. Make sure to label the steps in the process.

Cloud Dragons

by Pat Mora

What do you see
in the clouds so high?
What do you see in the sky?

Oh, I see dragons
that curl their tails
as they go slithering by.

What do you see
in the clouds so high?
What do you see? Tell me, do.

Oh, I see *caballitos*
that race the wind
high in the shimmering blue.

LEMON MOON
by Beverly McLoughland

On a hot and thirsty summer night,
The moon's a wedge of lemon light
Sitting low among the trees,
Close enough for you to squeeze
And make a moonade, icy-sweet,
To cool your summer-dusty heat.

Hurt No Living Thing
by Christina Rossetti

Hurt no living thing;
Ladybird, nor butterfly,
Nor moth with dusty wing,
Nor cricket chirping cheerily,
Nor grasshopper so light of leap,
Nor dancing gnat, nor beetle fat,
Nor harmless worms that creep.

Springtime

by Nikki Giovanni

in springtime the violets
grow in the sidewalk cracks
and the ants play furiously
at my gym-shoed toes
carrying off a half-eaten peanut
butter sandwich i had at lunch
and sometimes i crumble
my extra graham crackers
and on the rainy days i take off
my yellow space hat and splash
all the puddles on Pendry Street and not one
cold can catch me

Laughing Boy

by Richard Wright

In the falling snow
A laughing boy holds out his palms
Until they are white.

Author Study

Do you have a favorite selection? Make a note of the author's name and look for books by that author. You will probably enjoy other works by him or her.

Try It

- Find three or four works by one author.
- Read the book jackets or use the Internet to learn about the author's life to see what may have influenced his or her writing.
- Read the author's works.
- Compare topics, genres, and so on.
- Tell which work is your favorite and why.

Read this author study of Kathleen Krull.

Kathleen Krull

Kathleen Krull has written numerous biographies. "My interest in biography as a literary form comes from curiosity about the details of others' lives. To put it in a simple way, I'm nosy." Ms. Krull has written about many important people in history. Some of those people include musicians, writers, presidents, and athletes. My favorite books are in her Lives of... series.

Authors and Illustrators

Carey Armstrong-Ellis
The author and illustrator of *Prudy's Problem*, p. 232

Carey Armstrong-Ellis collects snow globes and funny salt and pepper shakers. Her daughters also collect things. They inspired her to write the story *Prudy's Problem*. Ms. Armstrong-Ellis painted the pictures for her book much later.   **Other books about collecting include *Let's Go Rock Collecting* and *Collecting Baseball Cards*.**

Michael Bania
The author and illustrator of *Kumak's Fish*, p. 88

Michael Bania taught for many years in an Inuit village. Ms. Bania saw how her students loved to hear the stories the elders told. She decided to write these stories so that all children may read them. She resides in Alaska where she continues to write.   **Another book by Michael Bania is *Kumak's House*.**

Joseph Bruchac
The author of *Pushing Up the Sky*, p. 344

As a young boy Joseph Bruchac loved reading and nature. Bruchac has traveled all over America listening to stories of different Native American tribes. He has always been a very careful listener.   **Joseph Bruchac has written many books; look for them at your library.**

Robert Casilla
The illustrator of *First Day in Grapes*, p. 206

Robert Casilla has illustrated many award-winning books. He uses models to help him illustrate people. Mr. Casilla even used himself as a model for Old Hoonch in *First Day in Grapes!* He lives in New York with his wife and two children.   **Mr. Casilla illustrates a series of picture books about important people in history.**

Suzanne Collins
The author of *When Charlie McButton Lost Power*, p. 32

Between writing for different Emmy-nominated television series, Suzanne Collins has written children's books. She wrote *Charlie McButton* after her own son found out he could have fun with things that didn't need power or to be plugged in, like his sister! **Ms. Collins has also written *The Underland Chronicles*, a middle-grade, fantasy series.**

Ron Fridell
The author of *Amazing Bird Nests*, p. 288

Ron Fridell lives in Tucson, Arizona, where there are lots of birds. "While I was writing *Amazing Bird Nests*, it was spring—nest-building time. And right outside the kitchen window on a plant hanger, a hummingbird was building her nest." **Mr. Fridell has also written about spiders, turtles, frogs, silkworms, scorpions, and snakes.**

Kathleen Krull
The author of *Supermarket*, p. 114

Kathleen Krull was fired from her job in the library when she was 15 years old—for reading too much! Her love of reading hasn't changed, and her love of music has greatly influenced her writing. She lives in San Diego, California, with her illustrating husband, Paul Brewer. **Ms. Krull has also written *M Is for Music* and *Lives of the Musicians*.**

Donna Latham
The author of *Seeing Stars*, p. 372

When she isn't connecting stars to make pictures in the sky, Donna Latham is writing. Her book *Fire Dogs* received the ASPCA Henry Bergh Children's Book Award with her Lhasa Apsa, Nikki, by her side. **Her other books include *Ellen Ochoa: Reach for the Stars!* and *Hurricane! The Galveston 1900 Night of Terror.***

Mike Lester
The illustrator of *When Charlie McButton Lost Power*, p. 32

Mike Lester has been writing and illustrating books for more than twenty years. Besides his children's books, Mr. Lester is also an editorial cartoonist for his local newspaper, *Rome News-Tribune*. He lives in Rome, Georgia, with his two children, two birds, and two dogs. **His latest book is *Cool Daddy Rat*.**

E. B. Lewis
The illustrator of *My Rows and Piles of Coins*, p. 146

As early as third grade, E. B. Lewis showed great artistic talent. For the illustrations in *My Rows and Piles of Coins*, Mr. Lewis won a Coretta Scott King Honor Award. About painting in his studio, Mr. Lewis says, "The music is blasting—everything from rap to classical to jazz. Paint is everywhere. It's not a bad way to make a living."

Tololwa Mollel
The author of *My Rows and Piles of Coins*, p. 146

Tololwa Mollel grew up in a small village in Tanzania, Africa. Mr. Mollel often went to the market with his grandmother. "It was the only time I got any money!" he says. "But the boy in the story is smarter than I was because he saved his money." **You may also want to read these other books by Mr. Mollel, *The Orphan Boy* and *Kele's Secret*.**

Wendell Minor
The illustrator of *A Symphony of Whales*, p. 394

Wendell Minor travels all over the world to research his books. When working with Jean Craighead George on *Snow Bear* and *Arctic Son*, he went to Barrow, Alaska. Those experiences helped him paint the pictures for *A Symphony of Whales*. Mr. Minor says, "What gives me satisfaction is bringing the world of nature to children."

L. King Pérez
The author of *First Day in Grapes,* p. 206

L. King Pérez has always been a reader. "I began reading with cereal boxes and 'Do Not Remove This Tag' on furniture." She based *First Day in Grapes* on her husband's experiences as a child in a migrant family. **Another book about children like Chico is *Calling the Doves.***

Steve Schuch
The author of *A Symphony of Whales,* p. 394

Steve Schuch first became interested in whales when a scientist who was also a musician came to his college. The musician played his cello along with recordings of whale songs. "That evening forever changed how I heard music and thought about whales," says Mr. Schuch.

David Small
The illustrator of *The Gardener,* p. 318

David Small illustrated the book his wife Sarah Stewart, wrote—*The Gardener.* He won a Caldecott Honor for his pictures in this book. Ms. Stewart and Mr. Small live in an old house along a river in Michigan where his studio is just a short walk away. **He has illustrated a series of books by Judith St. George about presidents, explorers, and inventors!**

Janet Stevens
The author/illustrator of *Tops and Bottoms,* p. 260

When Janet Stevens began writing *Tops and Bottoms,* the words just would not come to her, so she started by drawing the pictures. "Drawing pictures first of Bear and Hare helped me get to know them. As I dressed them up and knew their personalities, they started to talk. Then I could write the story." Ms. Stevens likes us to learn about the characters through her drawings. **Another book by Janet Stevens is *Coyote Steals the Blanket.***

Sarah Stewart
The author of *The Gardener*, p. 318

As a child, Sarah Stewart's favorite places were the library and her grandmother's garden. She loved quiet places where she could think and dream. At the library she would daydream with a book. "In my grandmother's garden, I could dig in the earth or cut a bouquet or simply lie down between the rows and listen to the silence." **Ms. Stewart has also written *The Library* and *The Journey*.**

Betty Tatham
The author of *Penguin Chick,* p. 180

Betty Tatham says, "I write mostly about things I like, and I love animals." She chose to write about emperor penguins because she found them interesting. "I liked the fact that the dad takes care of the egg and that the mother penguin finds her mate by listening to his voice. I liked the loving relationship both parents have with their chick." **Other books Ms. Tatham has written about animals *How Animals Shed Their Skin* and *How Animals Communicate.***

Ed Young
The author/illustrator of *What About Me?*, p. 62

Ed Young was born in Tienstin, China, and grew up in Shanghai and Hong Kong. The Chinese often pair words with their painting. Mr. Young agrees with that idea. "There are things that words do that pictures never can, and likewise, there are images that words can never describe." **Mr. Young has illustrated more than eighty children's books.**

Glossary

How to Use This Glossary

This glossary can help you understand and pronounce some of the words in this book. The entries in this glossary are in alphabetical order. There are guide words at the top of each page to show you the first and last words on the page. A pronunciation key is at the bottom of the following page. Remember, if you can't find the word you are looking for, ask for help or check a dictionary.

The entry word is in dark type. It shows how the word is spelled and how the word is divided into syllables.

The pronunciation is in parentheses. It also shows which syllables are stressed.

Part-of-speech labels show the function or functions of an entry word and any listed form of that word.

a·dore (ə dôr′), *VERB.* to love and admire someone very greatly: *She adores her mother.* ❏ *VERB.* **a·dores, a·dored, a·dor·ing.**

Sometimes, irregular and other special forms will be shown to help you use the word correctly.

The definition and example sentence show you what the word means and how it is used.

Aa

ant·ler (ant′lər), *NOUN.* a bony, branching growth on the head of a male deer, elk, or moose. Antlers grow in pairs and are shed once a year. ❏ *PLURAL* **ant·lers.**

antlers

anx·ious·ly (angk′shəs lē), *ADVERB.* uneasily; with fear of what might happen: *We looked anxiously at the storm clouds.*

ar·range (ə rānj′), *VERB.* to put things in a certain order: *She arranged the books on the library shelf.* ❏ *VERB* **ar·rang·es, ar·ranged, ar·rang·ing.**

Bb

bat (bat), *NOUN.* **1.** a small, flying mammal that comes out at night to feed: *Bats have sensitive ears.* **2.** a piece of wood or metal used for hitting the ball in baseball or softball.

bat 1.

bat·ter·y (bat′ ə rē), *NOUN.* a container filled with chemicals that produces electrical power: *We needed a battery for the flashlight.*

bay (bā), *NOUN.* a part of a sea or lake partly surrounded by land.

beau·ty (byü′tē), *NOUN.* the quality that pleases both the mind and the senses in art or nature.

bill (bil), *NOUN.* the beak of a bird.

bill

blew (blü), *VERB.* past tense of *blow.*

bliz·zard (bliz′ərd), *NOUN.* a blinding snowstorm with very strong, cold winds. ❑ *PLURAL* **bliz·zards.**

bloom (blüm), *VERB.* to have flowers; open into flowers; blossom: *Many plants are blooming early this spring.* ❑ *VERB* **blooms, bloomed, bloom·ing.**

blow (blō), *VERB.* **1.** to make air come out of your mouth. **2.** to move in the wind: *The leaves blew around the yard.* ❑ *VERB* **blows, blew, blow·ing.**

a	in hat	ėr	in term	ô	in order	ch	in child	ə	= a in about
ā	in age	i	in it	oi	in oil	ng	in long	ə	= e in taken
â	in care	ī	in ice	ou	in out	sh	in she	ə	= i in pencil
ä	in far	o	in hot	u	in cup	th	in thin	ə	= o in lemon
e	in let	ō	in open	u̇	in put	ᴛʜ	in then	ə	= u in circus
ē	in equal	ȯ	in all	ü	in rule	zh	in measure		

boom (büm), *VERB.* to speak in a loud, deep voice: *"All aboard!" the train conductor boomed.* ❑ *VERB* **booms, boomed, boom·ing.**

bot·tom (bot′əm), *NOUN.* the lowest part: *These berries at the bottom of the basket are crushed.*

bounce (bouns), *VERB.* to spring back after hitting something: *The ball bounced across the blacktop.* ❑ *VERB* **boun·ces, bounced, bounc·ing.**

bulb (bulb), *NOUN.* a round, underground part from which certain plants grow. Onions and tulips grow from bulbs. ❑ *PLURAL* **bulbs.**

bun·dle (bun′dl), *NOUN.* a number of things tied or wrapped together. ❑ *PLURAL* **bun·dles.**

but·ter·fly (but′ ər flī), *NOUN.* an insect with large, often brightly colored wings: *Her flower garden attracted many butterflies.* ❑ *PLURAL* **but·ter·flies.**

butterfly

Cc

car·pen·ter (kär′pən tər), *NOUN.* someone whose work is building and repairing things made of wood.

carpenter

car·pet·ma·ker (kär′pit māk ər), *NOUN.* A person who makes carpets and rugs for floors: *The carpetmaker sold us a blue carpet.*

chan·nel (chan′l), *NOUN.* a body of water joining two larger bodies of water: *The small channel was too narrow for the boat's passage.*

cheat (chēt), *VERB.* to deceive or trick someone; do business or play in a way that is not honest: *I hate to play games with someone who cheats.* ❑ *VERB* **cheats, cheat·ed, cheat·ing.**

chip (chip), *VERB.* to cut or break off a small thin piece of something: *I chipped the cup when I knocked it against the cupboard.* ❑ *VERB* **chips, chipped, chip·ping.**

clev·er (klev ′ər), ADJECTIVE. bright; intelligent; having a quick mind: *She is a clever girl to have solved that math problem.*

col·lec·tion (kə lek′shən), NOUN. a group of things gathered from many places and belonging together: *Our library has a large collection of books.*

collection

con·dense (kən dens′), VERB. when a gas condenses, it turns into a liquid, usually as a result of cooling: *On a hot day, water vapor condenses on the outside of a drinking glass.* ❑ VERB **con·dens·es, con·densed, con·dens·ing.**

con·serve (kən sėrv′), VERB. to save something from loss or waste: *Fixing a leaky faucet helps to conserve water.* ❑ VERB **con·serves, con·served, con·serv·ing.**

crate (krāt), NOUN. a large, open, usually wooden box: *We needed three crates to carry all the oranges.* ❑ PLURAL **crates.**

crop (krop), NOUN. plants grown for food: *Wheat, corn, and beans are major crops in the United States.* ❑ PLURAL **crops.**

crop

cud·dle (kud′l), VERB. to lie close and comfortably; curl up: *The two puppies cuddled together in front of the fire.* ❑ VERB **cud·dles, cud·dled, cud·dling.**

Dd

dan·ger·ous·ly (dān′jər əs lē), ADVERB. not safely: *The car drove dangerously close to the wall.*

di·gest (dī jest′), VERB. to break down food in the body so that nutrients are absorbed: *Your stomach and intestines help to digest the food you eat.* ❑ VERB **di·gests, di·gest·ed, di·gest·ing.**

dim (dim), *ADJECTIVE.* somewhat dark; not bright: *The light from the candle was too dim for reading.*

dis·solve (di zȯlv′), *VERB.* to break apart into tiny, often invisible pieces when mixed with liquid: *Sugar dissolves in water.* ❑ *VERB* **dis·solves, dis·solved, dis·solv·ing.**

doze (dōz), *VERB.* to sleep lightly; be half asleep: *After dinner, he dozed on the couch.* ❑ *VERB* **doz·es, dozed, doz·ing.**

Ee

e·nor·mous (i nôr′məs), *ADJECTIVE.* very, very large; huge: *Long ago, enormous animals lived on the Earth.*

enormous

er·rand (er′ənd), *NOUN.* a short trip that you take to do something: *She has errands to do downtown.* ❑ *PLURAL* **er·rands.**

ex·cit·ed·ly (ek sī′tid lē), *ADVERB.* with strong, lively feelings: *My heart beat excitedly as I opened the old trunk.*

Ff

flip·per (flip′ər), *NOUN.* one of the broad, flat body parts used for swimming by animals such as seals and penguins. ❑ *PLURAL* **flip·pers.**

flipper

fro·zen (frō′zn), *ADJECTIVE.* hardened with cold; turned into ice: *frozen sherbet.*

fu·el (fyü′ əl), *NOUN.* something that is used as a source of heat or energy, such as gasoline, coal, or wood: *The car wouldn't run because it was out of fuel.*

Gg

gas (gas), *NOUN.* a substance, such as air, that is neither a solid nor a liquid: *Sometimes balloons are filled with a gas called helium.*

gear (gir), *NOUN.* the equipment or clothing needed for a particular activity: *Their camping gear included tents, sleeping bags, and flashlights.*

gi·gan·tic (jī gan′ tik), *ADJECTIVE.* huge or enormous: *The gigantic footprints must have been made by an elephant.*

goo (gü), *NOUN.* a sticky or messy substance: *Wash that goo off your hands.*

Hh

hatch (hach), *VERB.* to come out of an egg: *One of the chickens hatched today.* ❏ *VERB* **hatch·es, hatched, hatch·ing.**

hatch

hu·mor (hyü′mər), *NOUN.* the ability to see or show the funny or amusing side of things: *Her sense of humor enabled her to joke about her problems.*

hun·ter (hun′ tər), *NOUN.* a person or animal who chases and kills animals for food: *Owls and eagles are hunters.* ❏ *PLURAL* **hun·ters.**

hunter

Ii

i·mag·ine (i maj′ən), *VERB.* to make a picture or idea of something in your mind: *We can hardly imagine life without cars.* ❏ *VERB* **i·mag·ines, i·mag·ined, i·mag·in·ing.**

im·pur·i·ty (im pyür′ ə tē), *NOUN.* something that makes a substance unclean: *Some water contains impurities such as dirt and garbage that make it unsafe to drink.* ❏ *PLURAL* **im·pur·i·ties.**

Kk

knead (nēd), *VERB.* to use your hands to press or mix together dough or clay: *After you mix the ingredients, knead the bread dough for five minutes.* ❏ *VERB* **kneads, knead·ed, knead·ing.**

knowl·edge (nol′ij), *NOUN.* what you know: *Gardeners have great knowledge of flowers.*

Ll

la·dle (lā′ dl), *NOUN.* a large spoon with a long handle and a deep bowl: *Dad used a ladle to serve the soup.*

ladle

lane (lān), *NOUN.* a narrow road or street: *We didn't see any cars as we walked down the lane to the old cottage.*

lan·guage (lan′gwij), *NOUN.* human speech, spoken or written: *Civilization would be impossible without language.* ❏ *PLURAL* **lan·guag·es.**

laun·dry (lȯn′ drē), **1.** *NOUN.* clothes, towels, and other such items that need to be washed or have just been washed: *One of my chores is folding the laundry.* **2.** *ADJECTIVE.* used for doing laundry: *The laundry basket was full of dirty clothes.*

laundry

la·zy (lā′zē), *ADJECTIVE.* not willing to work or move fast. *He lost his job because he was lazy.*

li·quid (lik′ wid), *NOUN.* a wet substance that you can pour: *The bottle of green liquid spilled all over the table.*

lurch (lėrch), *VERB.* to move in an unsteady, jerky way: *The passengers lurched forward when the bus came to a sudden stop.* ❏ *VERB* **lur·ches, lurched, lurch·ing.**

Mm

mar·ket·place (mär′kət plās′), *NOUN.* a place where people meet to buy and sell things: *The marketplace was very crowded.*

ma·te·ri·al (mə tir′ ē əl), *NOUN.* the substance from which something is made: *The Three Little Pigs used different materials to build their houses.* ❑ *PLURAL* **ma·te·ri·als.**

mel·o·dy (mel′ə dē), *NOUN.* a pleasing or easily remembered series of musical notes; tune.

mer·chant (mėr′chənt), *NOUN.* someone who buys and sells goods for a living: *Some merchants do most of their business with foreign countries.*

Nn

nar·ra·tor (nar′āt ər), *NOUN.* the person who tells the story or tale: *I was the narrator in the school play.*

Oo

o·ver·head (ō′vər hed′), *ADVERB.* over the head; on high; above: *The stars twinkled overhead.*

Pp

par·ka (pär′ kə), *NOUN.* a warm, heavy jacket with a hood: *If you go out in this cold weather, you should wear your parka.*

parka

part·ner (pärt′nər), *NOUN.* a member of a company or firm who shares the risks and profits of the business. ❑ *PLURAL* **part·ners.**

pat·tern (pat′ ėrn), *NOUN.* an arrangement or design: *The birthday cake was decorated with a pattern of balloons.* ❑ *PLURAL* **pat·terns.**

peck (pek), *VERB.* to strike with the beak: *The baby sparrow pecks at the egg.* ❑ *VERB* **pecks, pecked, peck·ing.**

plat·form (plat′ fôrm), *NOUN.* a flat, raised structure or surface: *He stepped up on the platform to give his speech.*

Glossary

459

plen·ty (plen'tē), NOUN. a full supply; all that you need; a large enough number or amount: *You have plenty of time to catch the train.*

plug (plug), NOUN. a device at the end of a wire that is put into an electrical outlet to make a connection with a source of electricity: *A plug has metal prongs.*

poke (pōk), VERB. to push with force against someone or something; jab: *He poked me in the ribs with his elbow.* ❑ VERB **pokes, poked, pok·ing.**

preen (prēn), VERB. to smooth or arrange the feathers with the beak. ❑ VERB **preens, preened, preen·ing.**

preen

Rr

rec·og·nize (rek'əg nīz), VERB. to identify: *recognizing a person from a*

description. ❑ VERB **rec·og·niz·es, rec·og·nized, rec·og·niz·ing.**

re·fresh·ing (ri fresh' ing) ADJECTIVE. having the ability to make something fresh again: *A refreshing breeze cooled us off.*

Ss

scat·ter (skat'ər), VERB. to separate and go in different directions: *The chickens scattered in fright when the truck honked at them.* ❑ VERB **scat·ters, scat·tered, scat·ter·ing.**

sec·tion (sek' shən), NOUN. a part or division of something: *I visited the children's section of the library.*

shelf (shelf), NOUN. a horizontal board on a wall or in a cupboard, used for holding or storing things: *Meg placed the books on the shelves.* ❑ PLURAL **shelves.**

shine (shīn), VERB. to give off light or reflect light; glow: *The candles on the cake shine for a moment before Rebecca blows them out.* ❑ VERB **shines, shone, shin·ing.**

shoe·lace (shü' lās), NOUN. a string or cord used for fastening a shoe: *The kindergartners practiced tying their shoelaces.* ❑ PLURAL **shoe·la·ces.**

show·er (shou′ər), *NOUN.* rain that lasts only a short time. ❑ *PLURAL* **show·ers.**

smirk (smėrk), *VERB.* to smile in a smug or knowing way: *After he scored the final goal, my brother smirked and bragged about winning.* ❑ *VERB* **smirks, smirked, smirk·ing.**

snug·gle (snug′əl), *VERB.* to lie closely and comfortably together; nestle; cuddle: *The kittens snuggled together in the basket.* ❑ *VERB* **snug·gles, snug·gled, snug·gling.**

snuggle

splen·did (splen′did), *ADJECTIVE.* very good; excellent: *James and his family had a splendid vacation in Colorado.*

spoil (spoil), **1.** *VERB.* to become bad or not good to eat: *The fruit spoiled because I kept it too long.* **2.** *VERB.* to injure the character or disposition of: *They spoiled her by always givig her what she wanted.* ❑ *VERB* **spoils, spoiled, spoil·ing.**

sprout (sprout), *VERB.* to produce new leaves, shoots, or buds; begin to grow: *Tulips sprout in the spring.* ❑ *VERB* **sprouts, sprout·ed, sprout·ing.**

sprout

stead·y (sted′ē), *ADJECTIVE.* firmly fixed; firm; not swaying or shaking: *This post is as steady as a rock.*

store (stôr), **1.** *NOUN.* a place where things are sold, as in *a grocery store* or *a toy store.* **2.** *VERB.* to put things away until they are needed: *We store the extra blankets in the closet during the summer.*

strain (strān), *VERB.* to draw tight; stretch too much: *The weight strained the rope.* ❑ *VERB* **strains, strained, strain·ing.**

Glossary

stray (strā), *VERB.* to lose your way; wander; roam: *Our dog has strayed off somewhere.* ❏ *VERB* **strays, strayed, stray·ing.**

sub·stance (sub′ stəns), *NOUN.* something that has weight and takes up space; matter: *Powders, liquids, and solids are substances.* ❏ *PLURAL* **sub·stan·ces.**

sup·plies (sə plīz′), *NOUN PLURAL.* the food and equipment necessary for an army exercise, camping trip, and so on.

sur·round (sə round′), *VERB.* to shut something in on all sides; encircle; enclose: *A high fence surrounded the field.* ❏ *VERB* **sur·rounds, sur·round·ed, sur·round·ing.**

sym·pho·ny (sim′fə nē), *NOUN.* a long, complicated musical composition for an orchestra.

Tt

tem·per·a·ture (tem′ pər ə chər), *NOUN.* The degree of heat or cold in something, usually measured by a thermometer: *The water temperature was too cold for swimming.*

term (tėrm), *NOUN.* a definite or limited time: *A president's term in office is four years.*

thou·sand (thou′znd), *NOUN* or *ADJECTIVE.* ten hundred; 1,000. ❏ *PLURAL* **thou·sands.**

thread (thred), *NOUN.* a very thin string made of strands of cotton, silk, wool, or nylon, spun and twisted together. *She sewed the sweater with cotton thread.*

thread

ton (tun), *NOUN.* a unit of weight equal to 2,000 pounds: *A small car weighs about one ton, and a minivan weighs about two tons.* ❏ *PLURAL* **tons.**

trade (trād), *VERB.* to exchange one thing for another: *Rita traded her blue crayon for a red one.* ❏ *VERB* **trades, tra·ded, tra·ding.**

twig (twig), *NOUN.* a small, thin branch of a tree or other woody plant: *The children collected small sticks and twigs to decorate their sandcastle.* ❏ *PLURAL* **twigs.**

twitch (twich), *VERB.* to make small, jerky movements: *The cat's tail twitched as he watched the bird outside the window.* ❑ *VERB* **twitch·es, twitch·ed, twitch·ing.**

Uu

un·wrap (un rap′), *VERB.* to open: *She unwrapped the gift.* ❑ *VERB* **un·wraps, un·wrapped, un·wrap·ping.**

Vv

va·ri·e·ty (və rī′ ə tē), *NOUN.* a selection of different things: *This market sells a wide variety of fruits and vegetables.*

vis·ion (vizh′ ən), *NOUN.* the ability to think ahead and plan: *Our group needs a leader with vision.*

Ww

warn (wôrn), *VERB.* to advise or caution: *The teacher warned us not to run in the hall.* ❑ *VERB* **warns, warned, warn·ing.**

wealth (welth), *NOUN.* riches; many valuable possessions; property: *people of wealth, the wealth of a city.*

wil·low (wil′ ō), *NOUN.* a tree with narrow leaves and thin branches that bend easily: *She liked to sit under the curved branches of the willow.*

wob·ble (wob′əl), *VERB.* to move unsteadily from side to side; shake; tremble: *The baby wobbled when she began to walk alone.* ❑ *VERB* **wob·bles, wob·bled, wob·bling.**

willow

Yy

yank (yangk), *VERB.* to pull with a sudden, sharp movement : *Keith yanked open the heavy door.* ❑ *VERB* **yanks, yanked, yank·ing.**

Unit 1

When Charlie McButton Lost Power

English	Spanish
bat	murciélago
battery	* batería
blew	estalló
plug	enchufe
vision	* visión
fuel	combustible
term	duración

What About Me?

English	Spanish
carpenter	* carpintero
carpetmaker	alfombrista
knowledge	conocimiento
marketplace	mercado
merchant	comerciante
plenty	mucho
straying	descarriando
thread	hilo

Kumak's Fish

English	Spanish
twitch	tirón
gear	aparejos
willow	sauce
yanked	arrastró
splendid	* espléndido
parka	* parka

Supermarket

English	Spanish
thousands	miles
traded	intercambiaban
variety	variedad
shelves	estantes
section	* sección
spoiled	echada a perder
laundry	lavandería
store	tienda

* English/Spanish Cognate: A **cognate** is a word that is similar in Spanish and has the same meaning in both languages.

My Rows and Piles of Coins

English	Spanish
arranged	ordené
bundles	paquetes
dangerously	peligrosamente
errands	recados
excitedly	con emoción
steady	estable
unwrapped	desenvolví
wobbled	me tambaleé

Unit 2

Penguin Chick

English	Spanish
cuddles	se arrima a
flippers	aletas
frozen	congelada
hatch	salir del cascarón
pecks	picotea
preen	atusa
snuggles	se acurruca

First Day in Grapes

English	Spanish
boomed	resonó
lane	callejuela
lurched	aceleró
bounced	brincaban
crates	canastas
smirked	sonrió despectivo
warned	aconsejó

Prudy's Problem

English	Spanish
butterflies	mariposas
collection	* colección
enormous	* enorme
scattered	desparramadas
shoelaces	cordones de zapatos
strain	doblarse

Tops & Bottoms

English	Spanish
bottom	parte de abajo
cheated	engañaste
clever	listo
crops	cosechas
lazy	perezoso
partners	socios
wealth	riqueza

Amazing Bird Nests

English	Spanish
material	* materiales
hunters	cazadoras
bill	pico
twigs	ramitas
tons	toneladas
platform	* plataformas
goo	baba

Unit 3

The Gardener

English	Spanish
beauty	belleza
blooming	floreciendo
bulbs	* bulbos
doze	me quedo dormido
humor	* humor
knead	amasar
recognizing	reconocer
showers	lluvias
sprouting	brotando

Pushing Up the Sky

English	Spanish
antlers	cuernos
imagined	* imaginar
languages	idiomas
narrator	* narrador
overhead	por arriba
(holes) poked	(agujeros) hechos

Seeing Stars

English	Spanish
shine	brillar
gas	* gas
gigantic	* gigantescas
dim	opacas
temperature	* temperatura
patterns	figuras
ladle	cucharón

A Symphony of Whales

English	Spanish
anxiously	ansiosamente
bay	bahía
blizzards	ventiscas
channel	canal
chipped	picaron
melody	* melodía
supplies	suministros
surrounded	rodeada
symphony	* sinfonía

Did a Dinosaur Drink This Water?

English	Spanish
substances	* sustancias
impurities	* impurezas
condenses	* se condensa
conserve	* conservar
digest	digerir
liquid	* líquida
refreshing	* refrescante
dissolve	* disuelve

Reading

1.0 Word Analysis, Fluency, and Systematic Vocabulary Development

Students understand the basic features of reading. They select letter patterns and know how to translate them into spoken language by using phonics, syllabication, and word parts. They apply this knowledge to achieve fluent oral and silent reading.

Decoding and Word Recognition

1.1 Know and use complex word families when reading (e.g., -ight) to decode unfamiliar words.
1.2 Decode regular multisyllabic words.
1.3 Read aloud narrative and expository text fluently and accurately and with appropriate pacing, intonation, and expression.

Vocabulary and Concept Development

1.4 Use knowledge of antonyms, synonyms, homophones, and homographs to determine the meanings of words.
1.5 Demonstrate knowledge of levels of specificity among grade-appropriate words and explain the importance of these relations (e.g., dog/mammal/ animal/living things).
1.6 Use sentence and word context to find the meaning of unknown words.
1.7 Use a dictionary to learn the meaning and other features of unknown words.
1.8 Use knowledge of prefixes (e.g., un-, re-, pre-, bi-, mis-, dis-) and suffixes (e.g., -er, -est, -ful) to determine the meaning of words.

2.0 Reading Comprehension

Students read and understand grade-level-appropriate material. They draw upon a variety of comprehension strategies as needed (e.g., generating and responding to essential questions, making predictions, comparing information from several sources). The selections in Recommended Literature, Kindergarten Through Grade Twelve illustrate the quality and complexity of the materials to be read by students. In addition to their regular school reading, by grade four, students read one-half million words annually, including a good representation of grade-level-appropriate narrative and expository text (e.g., classic and contemporary literature, magazines, newspapers, online information). In grade three, students make substantial progress toward this goal.

Structural Features of Informational Materials

2.1 Use titles, tables of contents, chapter headings, glossaries, and indexes to locate information in text.

Comprehension and Analysis of Grade-Level-Appropriate Text

2.2 Ask questions and support answers by connecting prior knowledge with literal information found in, and inferred from, the text.
2.3 Demonstrate comprehension by identifying answers in the text.
2.4 Recall major points in the text and make and modify predictions about forthcoming information.
2.5 Distinguish the main idea and supporting details in expository text.
2.6 Extract appropriate and significant information from the text, including problems and solutions.
2.7 Follow simple multiple-step written instructions (e.g., how to assemble a product or play a board game).

3.0 Literary Response and Analysis

Students read and respond to a wide variety of significant works of children's literature. They distinguish between the structural features of the text and literary terms or elements (e.g., theme, plot, setting, characters). The selections in Recommended Literature, Kindergarten Through Grade Twelve illustrate the quality and complexity of the materials to be read by students.

Structural Features of Literature

3.1 Distinguish common forms of literature (e.g., poetry, drama, fiction, nonfiction).

Narrative Analysis of Grade-Level-Appropriate Text

3.2 Comprehend basic plots of classic fairy tales, myths, folktales, legends, and fables from around the world.
3.3 Determine what characters are like by what they say or do and by how the author or illustrator portrays them.
3.4 Determine the underlying theme or author's message in fiction and nonfiction text.
3.5 Recognize the similarities of sounds in words and rhythmic patterns (e.g., alliteration, onomatopoeia) in a selection.
3.6 Identify the speaker or narrator in a selection.

Writing

1.0 Writing Strategies
Students write clear and coherent sentences and paragraphs that develop a central idea. Their writing shows they consider the audience and purpose. Students progress through the stages of the writing process (e.g., prewriting, drafting, revising, editing successive versions).

Organization and Focus
1.1 Create a single paragraph:
- **a.** Develop a topic sentence.
- **b.** Include simple supporting facts and details.

Penmanship
1.2 Write legibly in cursive or joined italic, allowing margins and correct spacing between letters in a word and words in a sentence.

Research
1.3 Understand the structure and organization of various reference materials (e.g., dictionary, thesaurus, atlas, encyclopedia).

Evaluation and Revision
1.4 Revise drafts to improve the coherence and logical progression of ideas by using an established rubric.

2.0 Writing Applications (Genres and Their Characteristics)
Students write compositions that describe and explain familiar objects, events, and experiences. Student writing demonstrates a command of standard American English and the drafting, research, and organizational strategies outlined in Writing Standard 1.0.

Using the writing strategies of grade three outlined in Writing Standard 1.0, students:
2.1 Write narratives:
- **a.** Provide a context within which an action takes place.
- **b.** Include well-chosen details to develop the plot.
- **c.** Provide insight into why the selected incident is memorable.

2.2 Write descriptions that use concrete sensory details to present and support unified impressions of people, places, things, or experiences.

2.3 Write personal and formal letters, thank-you notes, and invitations:
- **a.** Show awareness of the knowledge and interests of the audience and establish a purpose and context.
- **b.** Include the date, proper salutation, body, closing, and signature.

Written and Oral English Language Conventions

The standards for written and oral English language conventions have been placed between those for writing and for listening and speaking because these conventions are essential to both sets of skills.

1.0 Written and Oral English Language Conventions
Students write and speak with a command of standard English conventions appropriate to this grade level.

Sentence Structure
1.1 Understand and be able to use complete and correct declarative, interrogative, imperative, and exclamatory sentences in writing and speaking.

Grammar
1.2 Identify subjects and verbs that are in agreement and identify and use pronouns, adjectives, compound words, and articles correctly in writing and speaking.
1.3 Identify and use past, present, and future verb tenses properly in writing and speaking.
1.4 Identify and use subjects and verbs correctly in speaking and writing simple sentences.

Punctuation
1.5 Punctuate dates, city and state, and titles of books correctly.
1.6 Use commas in dates, locations, and addresses and for items in a series.

Capitalization
1.7 Capitalize geographical names, holidays, historical periods, and special events correctly.

Spelling
1.8 Spell correctly one-syllable words that have blends, contractions, compounds, orthographic patterns (e.g., *qu*, consonant doubling, changing the ending of a word from -*y* to -*ies* when forming the plural), and common homophones (e.g., *hair-hare*).
1.9 Arrange words in alphabetic order.

Listening and Speaking

1.0 Listening and Speaking Strategies

Students listen critically and respond appropriately to oral communication. They speak in a manner that guides the listener to understand important ideas by using proper phrasing, pitch, and modulation.

Comprehension

1.1 Retell, paraphrase, and explain what has been said by a speaker.

1.2 Connect and relate prior experiences, insights, and ideas to those of a speaker.

1.3 Respond to questions with appropriate elaboration.

1.4 Identify the musical elements of literary language (e.g., rhymes, repeated sounds, instances of onomatopoeia).

Organization and Delivery of Oral Communication

1.5 Organize ideas chronologically or around major points of information.

1.6 Provide a beginning, a middle, and an end, including concrete details that develop a central idea.

1.7 Use clear and specific vocabulary to communicate ideas and establish the tone.

1.8 Clarify and enhance oral presentations through the use of appropriate props (e.g., objects, pictures, charts).

1.9 Read prose and poetry aloud with fluency, rhythm, and pace, using appropriate intonation and vocal patterns to emphasize important passages of the text being read.

Analysis and Evaluation of Oral and Media Communications

1.10 Compare ideas and points of view expressed in broadcast and print media.

1.11 Distinguish between the speaker's opinions and verifiable facts.

2.0 Speaking Applications (Genres and Their Characteristics)

Students deliver brief recitations and oral presentations about familiar experiences or interests that are organized around a coherent thesis statement. Student speaking demonstrates a command of standard American English and the organizational and delivery strategies outlined in Listening and Speaking Standard 1.0.

Using the speaking strategies of grade three outlined in Listening and Speaking Standard 1.0, students:

2.1 Make brief narrative presentations:

    a. Provide a context for an incident that is the subject of the presentation.

    b. Provide insight into why the selected incident is memorable.

    c. Include well-chosen details to develop character, setting, and plot.

2.2 Plan and present dramatic interpretations of experiences, stories, poems, or plays with clear diction, pitch, tempo, and tone.

2.3 Make descriptive presentations that use concrete sensory details to set forth and support unified impressions of people, places, things, or experiences.

Acknowledgments

Text

32: *When Charlie McButton Lost Power* by Suzanne Collins and illustrated by Mike Lester. Text copyright © 2005 by Suzanne Collins. Illustrations copyright © 2005 by Mike Lester. Published by arrangement with G.P. Putnam's Sons, a division of Penguin Young Readers Group, a member of Penguin Group (USA) Inc. All rights reserved.

62: *What About Me?* by Ed Young. Copyright © 2002 by Ed Young. Published by arrangement with Philomel Books, a division of Penguin Young Readers Group, a member of Penguin Group (USA) Inc. All rights reserved.

88: *Kumak's Fish: A Tall Tale From the Far North* by Michael Bania. Text and illustrations © 2004 by Michael Bania. Reprinted by permission of Graphic Arts Center Publishing Company.

114: Text copyright © 2001 by Kathleen Krull. Illustrations copyright © 2001 by Melanie Hope Greenberg. All rights reserved. Reprinted from *Supermarket* by permission of Holiday House, Inc.

146: From *My Rows and Piles of Coins* by Tololwa M. Mollel. Text copyright © 1999 by Tololwa M. Mollel. Illustrations copyright © 1999 by E.B. Lewis. Reprinted by permission of Clarion Books, a division of Houghton Mifflin Company. All rights reserved.

168: "Solitude" from *Now We Are Six* by A.A. Milne, illustrated by E.H. Shepard, copyright 1927 by E.P. Dutton, renewed © 1955 by A.A. Milne. Used by permission of Dutton Children's Books, A Division of Penguin Young Readers Group, A Member of Penguin Group (USA) Inc., 345 Hudson Street, New York, NY 10014. All rights reserved.

169: From *Up the Windy Hill* by Aileen Fisher. Copyright © 1953, 1981 Aileen Fisher. Used by permission of Marian Reiner on behalf of the Boulder Public Library Foundation, Inc.

170: "Money" by Richard W. Armour from *For Partly Proud Parents: Light Verse About Children,* with an introduction by Phillis McGinley, 1950. Reprinted by permission.

171: From *Thematic Poetry: Transportation* by Betsy Franco. Scholastic Inc./Teaching Resources. Copyright © 2001 by Betsy Franco. Reprinted by permission.

180: *Penguin Chick* by Betty Tatham. Text copyright © 2002 by Betty Tatham. Illustrations copyright © 2002 Helen Davie. Used by permission of HarperCollins Publishers.

196: *Seeds, Stems, and Stamens* by Susan E. Goodman and photographs by Michael J. Doolittle. Text copyright © 2001 by Susan E. Goodman. Photographs copyright © 2001 by Michael J. Doolittle. Reprinted with the permission of Millbrook Press, a division of Lerner Publishing Group, Inc. All rights reserved. No part of this excerpt may be used or reproduced in any manner whatsoever without the prior written permission of Lerner Publishing Group, Inc.

206: *First Day in Grapes*, text copyright © 2002 by L. King Pérez, illustrations © 2002 by Robert Casilla. Rights arranged with Lee & Low Books Inc., New York, NY 10016.

232: From *Prudy's Problem and How She Solved It* by Carey Armstrong-Ellis. Published by Harry N. Abrams, Inc. Reprinted by permission.

260: *Tops and Bottoms*, copyright © 1995 by Janet Stevens, reprinted by permission of Harcourt, Inc. This material may not be reproduced in any form or by any means without the prior written permission of the publisher.

280: "The Hare and the Tortoise" from *Aesop's Fables* selected and illustrated by Michael Hague. Specially edited text © 1985 by Henry Holt and Company. Reprinted by permission of Henry Holt and Company, LLC.

302: From *A Journey Into Adaptation with Max Axiom, Super Scientist* by Agnieszka Biskup, illustrated by Cynthia Martin and Barbara Schulz. Copyright © 2007 by Capstone Press. All rights reserved. Reprinted by permission.

306: "Ants" reprinted with the permission of Atheneum Books for Young Readers, an imprint of Simon & Schuster Children's Publishing Division from *Fireflies at Midnight* by Marilyn Singer. Text copyright © 2003 Marilyn Singer.

307: "The Sure-Footed Shoe Finder" reprinted with the permission of Atheneum Books for Young Readers, an imprint of Simon & Schuster Children's Publishing Division from *Here's What You Do When You Can't Find Your Shoe* by Andrea Perry. Text copyright © 2003 Andrea Perry.

308: "Third-Grade Genius," from *Fearless Fernie: Hanging Out with Fernie & Me* by Gary Soto, copyright © 2002 by Gary Soto. Used by permission of G.P. Putnam's Sons, A Division of Penguin Young Readers Group, A Member of Penguin Group (USA) Inc., 345 Hudson Street, New York, NY 10014. All rights reserved.

318: *The Gardener* by Sarah Stewart, pictures by David Small. Text copyright © 1997 by Sarah Stewart. Pictures copyright © 1997 by David Small. Reprinted by permission of Farrar, Straus and Giroux, LLC.

344: "Pushing Up the Sky," from *Pushing Up the Sky* by Joseph Bruchac, copyright © 2000 by Joseph Bruchac. Used by permission of Dial Books for Young Readers, A Division of Penguin Young Readers Group, A Member of Penguin Group (USA) Inc., 345 Hudson Street, New York, NY 10014. All rights reserved.

358: Reprinted with the permission of Simon & Schuster Books for Young Readers, an imprint of Simon & Schuster Children's Publishing Division from *When the World Was Young* by Margaret Mayo, illustrated by Louise Brierly. Text copyright © 1995 Margaret Mayo. Illustrations copyright © 1995 Louise Brierly.

386: Excerpt from *Comets, Stars, the Moon, and Mars*, copyright © 2007 by Douglas Florian, reprinted by permission of Harcourt, Inc. This material may not be reproduced in any form or by any means without the prior written permission of the publisher.

394: *A Symphony of Whales*, text copyright © 1999 by Steve Schuch, reprinted by permission of Harcourt, Inc.

412: Reprinted from "He Listens to Whales" by E. Shan Correa, from the May 1991 issue of *Ranger Rick* ® magazine, with the permission of the publisher, The National Wildlife Federation ®. Copyright © 1991 by the National Wildlife Federation.

422: *Did a Dinosaur Drink This Water?* by Robert E. Wells. Text copyright © 2006 by Robert E. Wells. Originally published in hardcover and softcover by Albert Whitman & Company. Used with permission. All rights reserved.

Antonyms

Synonyms

Base Words

Prefixes

Suffixes

Context Clues

Word Families

Compound Words

Homographs

Homonyms

Homophones

Dictonary

Thesaurus

A Vocabulary Handbook

Antonyms

Antonyms are words that have opposite meanings. *Same* and *different* are antonyms.

Same

Antonyms can be used to contrast two things. Antonyms help readers understand differences.

Different

Synonyms

Synonyms are words that have the same meaning or similar meanings. *Loud* and *noisy* are synonyms.

Loud

Knowing and using synonyms can help make your writing more interesting. Look in a thesaurus to find synonyms.

Noisy

Base Words

A base word is a word that cannot be broken down into smaller words or word parts. *Cover* and *motion* are base words.

Cover

Motion

Knowing the meaning of a base word can help you understand the meanings of longer words.

Prefixes

A prefix is a word part that can be added to the beginning of a base word. In the word *uncover, un-* is a prefix.

Cover

Uncover

Knowing the meaning of a prefix can help you figure out the meaning of a new word.

Common Prefixes and Their Meanings

un-	not
re-	again, back
in-	not
dis-	not, opposite of
pre-	before

Suffixes

A suffix is a word part added to the end of a base word. In the word *motionless*, *-less* is a suffix.

Motion

Motionless

Common Suffixes and Their Meanings

-able	can be done
-ment	action or process
-less	without
-tion	act, process

Knowing how a suffix changes a word can help you figure out the meaning of a new word.

Context Clues

Read the words before and after a word that you don't know to help you make sense of it.

I couldn't decide what to wear! The red, blue, green, or fuchsia dress?

Word Families

Word families are related words that have the same base word. *Sign, signal,* and *signature* belong to the same word family. They all have the base word *sign*.

Sign

Signature

Signal

If you know the base words, you may be able to figure out the meanings of words related to it.

Compound Words

Compound words are words made of two smaller words. *Sandbox* and *ladybug* are compound words.

sand + **box** = **sandbox**

Look for smaller words that you already know in unfamiliar words.

lady + **bug** = **ladybug**

Multiple-Meaning Words

Multiple-meaning words are words that can have different meanings depending on how they are used.

Homographs

Homographs are words that are spelled the same but have different meanings. They may be pronounced the same way or differently.

Lead

Lead

Read the words before and after a homograph to discover its meaning and pronunciation. Check a dictionary to be sure.

Homonyms

Homonyms are words that are spelled the same and sound the same, but they have different meanings.

Seal

Seal

You can figure out the meaning of a homonym by reading the words around it.

Homophones

Homophones are words that sound the same, but they are spelled differently and they have different meanings.

Hair

Hare

Homophones might be confusing when *you* hear them being read aloud. Pay attention to the words before and after the homophone to find its meaning.

Understanding
Homographs, Homonyms, and Homophones

	Pronunciation	Spelling	Meaning
Homographs	may be the same or different	same	different
Homonyms	same	same	different
Homophones	same	different	different

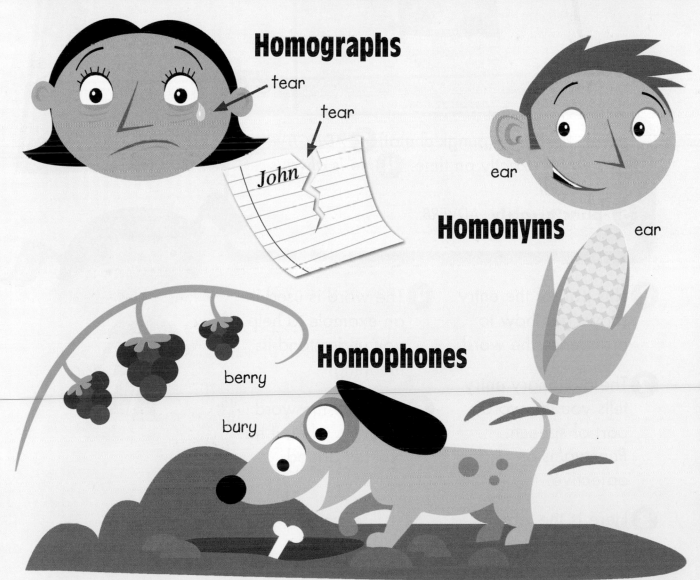

Homographs

tear

tear

John

ear

Homonyms

ear

berry

Homophones

bury

Dictionary

A dictionary is a book that explains the words of our language. The words in a dictionary are in alphabetical order.

punc·tu·al ❶ (pungk'chu al) ❷ *ADJECTIVE* ❸ prompt, exactly on time. ❹ *He is always punctual.* ❺ **-punc'tu·al·ly** *ADVERB.*

❶ This part of the entry shows you how to pronounce the word.

❷ The dictionary entry tells you the word's part of speech. *Punctual* is an adjective.

❸ Here is the word's definition.

❹ The word is used in an example to help you understand its meaning.

❺ See how the word changes when it has a suffix added.

Thesaurus

A thesaurus is a book of synonyms. The words in a thesaurus are in alphabetical order.

cute
adjective
attractive, appealing, amusing, charming, adorable, enchanting.

Keep a thesaurus handy when you write. It can help you find just the right word.

Spot is so cute!

SPOT

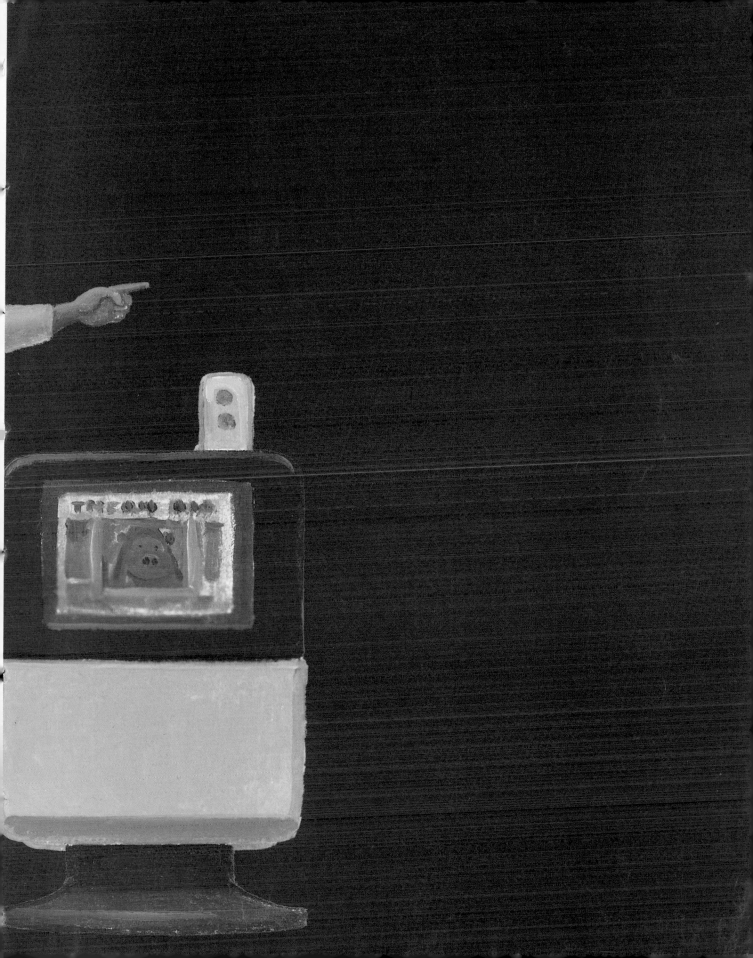